Advance Praise for Diary of an Anorexic Girl

I found this story eye-opening and hopeful, teaching
a lesson of love, forgiveness and hope to parents
and young people everywhere, while experiencing
some very real issues in life. Highly recommended.

Adrienne Liesching,
The Benjamin Gate

Morgan Menzie writes the most believable and real-
istic book about teenage girls I've ever read.
Honestly examining what every teen girl experiences
as she goes through a discovery process with
boys, self-image, jealousies, dieting, getting
noticed, and most importantly, anorexia, this book
speaks to every girl's heart. Read it. It will touch you
deeply and change you forever.

Libby Hodges, Jump 5

I was moved by Morgan's accurate and harrowing portrayal of the insidious nature of living with an eating disorder. Her writing illuminates the twists and distortions that one's mind can take in trying to obtain an illusory perfection. . . . This is important reading for parents, teachers, counselors and all young persons coping with living in a world that creates unreal expectations.

Karen A. Silien, Ph.D.
Licensed Psychologist
and Vice-President of
the Eating Disorders
Coalition of
Tennessee, Inc.

. . . Morgan has written a powerful book that reaches into what many view as an aberration, Christian young women dealing with a serious self-deprecating disease. She brings sagacity into the phenomenon by showing how a healthy Christian girl can fall susceptible to the horrors of anorexia and the miracle that comes when healing begins. I believe this book will be a tremendous source of insight, inspiration and healing for all who read it.

Lisa Kimmey,
Out of Eden

Diary of an Anorexic Girl

by Morgan Menzie

Published by
THOMAS NELSON
Since 1798

www.thomasnelson.com

Diary of an Anorexic Girl: Based on a True Story
Copyright © 2003 by Morgan Menzie

Published by W Publishing Group, a Thomas Nelson Company. P.O. Box 141000, Nashville, Tennessee 37214

Cover Design: Pointsize Associates, Glasgow, Scotland

Page Design: Book and Graphic Design, Nashville, Tennessee

Acquisitions Editor: Kate Etue

Editorial Staff: Beth Ann Patton, Jenny Eaton, Elizabeth Kea, Corinne Hyde

Scriptures quoted from *The Holy Bible, New Century Version,* copyright © 1987, 1988, 1991 by W Publishing Group, a division of Thomas Nelson, Inc. Used by permission.

Library of Congress Cataloging-in-Publication Data

Menzie, Morgan.
    Diary of an anorexic girl / Morgan Menzie.
      p. cm.
    Summary: A young girl keeps a diary recording her struggles with anorexia.
    ISBN-10: 0-8499-4405-8
    ISBN-13: 978-0-8499-4405-5
    [1. Anorexia nervosa—Fiction. 2. Diaries—Fiction. 3. Conduct of life—Fiction.] I. Title.
PZ7.M5318 Di 2002
[Fic]—dc21   2002013629

Printed and bound in the United States of America

07 RRD 9

For Marcelle,
  Whose love of God continually amazes me and whose gentle heart can never be captured in words.

And for Rachel,
  Who can take anything I throw at her and who will remain forever young.

DISCLAIMER

I wrote this book for me, as selfish as that sounds. It became my own form of therapy. The only way to overcome the past is to jump into it head first and come up clean. I baptized myself in the memories. But you should know that my story has been fictionalized. No, not all the characters in this novel are fictional. I'm not that brilliant; my creativity stops just short of plausibility. Most, with the exception of one or two individuals (who, if I had my way, I would bring to life) are real. Names have been changed, with the exception of Oreo the cat.

Speaking of names, I toyed with the idea of using my real name for the main character—for about two seconds. Then I vetoed that, for I've always wanted to make up a name for myself. But, if you would feel better thinking of Blythe as *Morgan,* you may take a pen and neatly cross out every "Blythe." I don't mind, really.

So when it comes down to it, this is my life. What you are reading really happened to me, just not in exact detail, because my memory is not, as they say, that of an elephant's. If you are so tormented by the mystery of what is real and what is not and as a result feel your black-and-white world slipping in to gray, 1) don't take yourself so seriously and 2) realize that I don't even remember what's real and what's not at this point.

Like I said, I wrote this for myself but the second the writing was done, it became yours. The moment I had finished saying what I had to say, it left me and sought you out. So read it with the knowledge that it was meant for you.

—Morgan Menzie

ACKNOWLEDGEMENTS

First and foremost I would like to thank Kate Etue, my editor and friend who helped me spin my thoughts into words. Kate, you had no reason to believe in me, but you took a chance anyway.

I'd also like to publicly acknowledge my brother, Craig. He does not, in fact, appear in the book. He was in college at the time these things happened to me, and I did not devise a way for him to enter the picture. My mind only stretches so far. But Craig, you know I love you!

I must thank "Liz." You know who you are. You are very gracious to allow me to turn you into the villain. Thanks for being the kid who always made fun of me; it turned into great material! And reader, I'd like to add that "Liz" turned out very well and is a lovely person whom I am proud to call my friend.

"Owen," you know I love you, buddy. That fact that there isn't an ounce of meanness in you was just too tempting. I had to make you a *little* shady. Call it the mischievous writer in me, but I wanted to see how you would be with a mean streak.

9.1.95

To Blythe,

Happy Birthday—thirteen is a happy age, so enjoy it! This journal is for you to write your life down in, and don't let anybody tell you that you are too young to know what you know. You've always been a bright one, from the time you opened your blue eyes and took in the world. You might be young, but you will never be simple.

Keep smiling darling, and never forget that Grandma and I love you.

Pa

1995

9.1.95

This is ridiculous really. I don't know who I think is going to read this, but I feel encouraged when an audience is listening.

Mom always says I have a flare for the dramatics. It's usually derogatory, but in my infinite wisdom I have turned it into a motto for life. You have to admit—if you were real you'd want me to talk to you directly. I would hate to exclude, so rather than risk hurting feelings (real or imaginary), I will include you in my narrative. Mom also says I over-analyze things, but I don't think so at all, and since you are my imaginary audience I have decided that you absolutely agree with me.

My grandpa gave me this journal and told me to start it today. Why, I don't know. Old people always have their reasons. He made the leather cover with my initials in the corner— in case you can't see it for yourself. He's from the country, or used to be before he moved to be closer to us, so homemade gifts are his specialty. I can't tell you how many tables and chests and shelves with pegs to hang keys on we've collected over the years.

All he said was, "Blythe, I want you to have this to write your life down in."

That's it; that's all he said before he began to whistle some old twangy hymn. For a man who could talk the bark off a tree, this was an abruptly short conversation, and perfectly suited for me.

So left with no guidance, here goes . . .

9.2.95

Well, gotta love seventh grade. I know this is supposed to be the time of my life, or is that high school . . . or college? It never really held much excitement for me—I've always been too smart for my age. Who would have thought intelligence a hindrance? Anyway, I feel absolutely awkward. The worst part is that I was born awkward *and* with foresight. I can see that my awkwardness will not blossom into some beautiful uniqueness—it will progress from awkwardness to homeliness to mediocrity.

Diane met me at the door to our first period. I wish I could carpool with her instead of horrible Liz, who always calls me a boy because of my short hair. I like my hair, or did before she made fun of it. I almost made it to school without crying this time . . . almost.

Anyway, Diane and I had a terrifically wretched first day. For one thing, first period is our only class together. That leaves six hours without my best friend. Oliver isn't even with me. He's my best friend other than Diane and he might as well have transferred for the amount of time I see him. It's horrible the way we are tragically separated and must suffer quietly while doomed to a solitary existence. Mom thinks I'm too melodramatic, but I just do whatever it takes to get me through the day—life should always be as exciting as possible.

Oh, speaking of drama, I saw Laurie picking at her food in lunch today. Diane and I watched her, and she hardly ate anything at all. The other girls noticed too, but of course Liz didn't pick on *her*. Maybe she just has a thing with short hair. I don't understand how you couldn't eat your food when it's taco day! At least pick a day like barbecue or fish triangles; but to dishonor the tacos and that apple crispito is just wrong. (I am patiently waiting for my taste buds to grow cultivated, but until then I will savor my greasy tacos and refried beans.)

Well, I'm rambling, and one thing that I've learned since joining the eighth grade is to make everything as short and sweet as possible. You blend in better that way.

9.21.95

I'd do anything to escape this world where everything is based on coolness and how loud you can pray. It's really become a pain ever since our middle school principal gave us the talk on making our faith our own rather than the adopted attitude of our parents. She might as well have said, "Howl at the moon," the way everyone is competing to "out-pray" each other. Maybe there's something wrong with me; I'm less than thrilled about all this independent faith stuff. Diane's jumped on the bandwagon, too. She does a devotional every day and writes pages and pages on the verses she's read. I don't think I'm that good of a Christian.

So instead of all this ranting, I'm going to live in the forest somewhere in the hollow of a big tree trunk and scrawl my brilliant, albeit agnostic, writings on its bark. And someday some wandering traveler will discover me and my tree full of words, and I will become a famous writer, and everybody in this school will still be ranting and raving.

9.28.95

Okay, here's the update on Laurie. Oliver won't even listen to me talk about her peculiar habits because he says it's not "guy stuff." And Diane is too religious to need this kind of excitement and too good to crave this kind of gossip. So I have undertaken the task of Laurie Mason's surveillance. Here's how she panned out for the week:

Monday:

No snack at break (new trend, normally she at least eats pretzels)

Half a bowl of tomato soup (no crackers as usual) for lunch

Nothing before soccer practice (I could never do that; I'm starving by three.)

Tuesday:

No snack (She thinks she's so cool.)

Salad at lunch (Actually just lettuce, no dressing—rabbit food, Mom calls it.)

Nothing before practice (I don't know how she does it! The guys are certainly noticing her more. Hmm . . .)

Note to self: See if you can skip snack tomorrow—or just eat pretzels if desperate.

10.5.95

New month—blah

> "Lowborn men are but a breath, the highborn are but a lie; if weighed on a balance, they are nothing; together they are only one breath."
>
> PSALM 62:9

I wish I could take Laurie Mason, tack a sign reading "highborn" to her back, and lead her to the river for baptizing! But then I guess I'd have to jump in after her. It's so unfair. I couldn't eat just pretzels today; I had to have a Coke, too. I've always been told I'm a strong-willed person—why can't I put it to good use?

I don't know why these journal entries come out so devastatingly depressing. I've always thought of myself as a happy person. I guess what's going on in my head is considerably less lighthearted than I choose to show people. Go figure.

Back to Laurie:

Diane says I'm very perceptive to notice all the things I have about her. I wonder if Diane is perceptive of me? Oliver sure isn't. I don't think it even registers with him that Diane and I are female. If Diane does notice what I'm up to maybe her best-friendedness will blind her to the whole truth. Great, I sound like the villain from a comic book: best friend by day, evil agnostic by night. Of course, I guess I've always been the overpowering one of the two of us. She hates conflict, so maybe she'll just pray for me quietly and leave me to do as I wish.

(Evil laugh.)

Thursday:

Water during snack (She's begun to drink an excessive amount. Could this be a trick I have not yet learned?)

Wasn't at lunch—said she was running errands for Mr. Linton. (Doubtful)

Ran an extra mile in soccer today because "I'm just not tired I guess." (She looked like she was about to keel over.)

Note to self: Discovered a new way to measure Laurie's decline/my progress—how much her soccer socks slide down during practice. Hers began right below the knee and now hit three-fourths down the shin. Mine have yet to begin their descent, but I feel hopeful.

10.10.95

Mean Liz ought to know better by now. I'd begun to ignore her taunts, and it had worked pretty well so far, but yesterday was the last straw. We were all waiting outside to be picked up from school when she started in.

"Hey, Blythe, turn your head to the side. Guys, doesn't she look just like a boy from that angle? . . . What are you looking at me like that for? I was just kidding."

Me in an unusually calm voice: "I don't think it's very funny."

"Oh well, what do you know? *They* all laughed. Don't look at me like that. I bet you're going to tell your mom when she picks us up, aren't you? Guys, she always tells her mom."

"Liz, please shut up."

"Whoa, a little sensitive are we? Hey, Blythe, do your Elvis impression. Guys, I swear, when she's about to smile her mouth curls up just like Elvis, and the hair just completes it. Come on, Blythe, do it. Do it. Come on, do it, Blythe."

"Liz, just shut up! I never want to talk to you ever again . . . Don't say another word! Stay out of my life! Do you hear me? Stay away from me!"

With that I stalked off to the far end of the sidewalk and to my dismay, began to cry. It would have been fine if I could have held it all in until I got home, but it was just too much. People always say kids can be cruel, but why does it have to happen to me?

Nobody talked on the way home, despite my mom continually asking me what's wrong. I just kept quiet, letting Liz live in fear.

I had made up my mind not to tell Mom. I don't know why, but Liz had pushed our battle to a level beyond parental control. I will freeze her out of my life. Not so much as a glance will pass between us. As far as I am concerned, she doesn't exist.

　　　　　　　　　　　　MORGAN MENZIE

10.13.95

There's a war raging, and Oliver and Diane are on my side. They came over last night to do homework and questioned me on my silence over the last few days. I filled them in on the scene between Liz and me, though doubtless they had already heard. News travels fast.

They listened in silence except for the occasional joking remark by Oliver to try to lift me out of my grim mood. In the end, Diane, though a little taken aback by my anger toward Liz, says she's going to stand by me. She refuses to contribute to the freeze-out, but she admits that what happened was not right and understands my point of view completely. Oliver thinks it's hilarious. He just kept shaking his head and muttering "Girls, girls . . . I don't get it." Surprisingly, I don't mind that he takes it lightly—that's just him. As long as he's on my side he can laugh it up all he wants.

So I have now expanded the game from two to four.

It's three against one; let's see who wins.

10.25.95

If I were a person who believed in the capacity to hate, I would hate Laurie Mason! I've been so preoccupied with ignoring Liz that I completely forgot about my other little game of observing Laurie. I think I might just abandon it altogether. I've discovered life is sweeter without the hassle.

Diane and I had the most wonderful weekend. One that would have been ruined if I had followed Laurie's unspoken rules and let my evil side take over. Friday night we walked from Diane's house to the football game. Because we hadn't spent much time together in ages and we weren't much interested in the game anyway, we got snow cones and walked around the grassy knoll to the side of the bleachers. (I bet Laurie didn't get a snow cone. I bet she didn't have any fun, either!)

After the game, we went back to Diane's house and watched *French Kiss* (it had to be a romantic comedy, of course), accompanied by popcorn, and I didn't care in the slightest that it was way past eight, which is when I decided I would quit eating each day. The next day, after a long serious discussion about which boy I thought might be my soulmate and hers (Diane never likes anybody, so I have to create my own fun), we walked to the gas station and bought ice cream bars and lay out in the field, wishing Christmas vacation were here. Actually, *I* was wishing it were here. I will forever be the only person in the universe who likes winter best.

10.30.95

Diane and I have been best friends since kindergarten, and I wouldn't have it any other way. Oliver and I didn't become friends until second grade when he sat across from me and made faces in Mrs. Reynold's class, so Diane gets seniority. She knows everything about me—or almost everything—and we've practically been sisters since the first day of school. We're quite opposites though, which I suppose suits the friendship. She's quiet, the best listener, and the most generous person I have ever met. I'm loud and obnoxious at times and I have a selfish streak that makes me stingy with anyone but her. She's also smaller than I am and blonde and lanky. I'm kinda tall, at least for my age, and I have plain-old brown hair that is too thick to do anything with but chop off (although it's been getting longer, not that it has lessened the teasing with Liz). I have blue eyes; she has green. I have freckles, glasses, and braces while she has none of these things.

Although Diane has essentially everything I want—except my blue eyes (those I like)—I have never been jealous of her. Well, maybe just a little and only for about four seconds at the most. We're too much the same person for that. Whatever is good for her is good for me. That's the way we work. In fact, I don't think I would be the person I am now without her. I know this digression is cheesy and sentimental, but it all goes back to my point. If Diane doesn't worry about how she looks or what she eats, and I already know she's an awesome person, why should I be obsessing over what Laurie-I'm-too-cool-for-everyone does?

Note to self: Ignore Laurie Mason with all my might.

11.2.95

I know I said I wasn't going to pay any attention to Laurie, but things aren't looking so good.

We were sitting in the locker room after the game last night. It was just me and her, 'cause everyone else had taken their stuff with them to the field. I tried to ignore her; I really did. But she was changing, and I turned to look away but found myself facing the mirror with her image in reverse. She was huddled in the corner trying not to be seen. It was horrible. Her ribs were sticking out and it looked painful to breathe, like the effort to expand and contract took too much out of her.

I looked away as quickly as I saw, but my gasp gave me away. She deftly pulled her shirt over her head and turned around to look at me. I could feel her eyes on my back.

"Please don't tell anyone."

"What?"

"Please don't tell anyone what you saw."

"What do you mean? I didn't see anything."

"Blythe, come on, who are we kidding? We've been watching each other since the season started. I won't tell anyone about you, if you won't tell anyone about me."

This shocked me. I didn't know she had been watching me! And what did she mean she wouldn't tell anyone about me?

"There's nothing wrong with me, Laurie. But do you want to talk to me about anything?"

"Oh don't give me that, Blythe. You're in the same boat as I am, just a little behind. Don't pretend you're all high and mighty. I'm lucky, my parents are getting a divorce and don't have time to keep their eye on me, but a few words from me to your mom or dad, and you'd be in trouble."

"Laurie, I don't know what—"

MORGAN MENZIE

"Just stop it, and swear you won't say anything, not to any-one. Not even to Oliver or Diane, and I'll swear the same."

Not really knowing what I was doing I took her bony pinky in mine and swore not to tell a soul.

I don't know what I've gotten myself into.

11.24.95

Thanksgiving Break

It's been three weeks since I promised Laurie I wouldn't tell her secret. I've watched her get smaller and smaller by the day. I can barely compare our socks anymore without feeling guilty for somehow contributing to her problem. Like I promised, I haven't told anyone—including Diane and Oliver. Oliver asked me why I'd all of a sudden gone so quiet on the subject of Laurie. I just said I thought he wasn't interested in all that girl stuff, and he gave it up.

It's Thanksgiving. Oliver and Diane and I are going Christmas shopping tomorrow. I think this is going to be a pretty low-key holiday. None of the relatives are coming into town, which is a relief. Of course, this just means they're saving up their frequent-flyer miles for Christmas, but I'm not going to think about that.

I've given myself a resolution for this week: Do not eat like Laurie. This is supposed to be a time of happiness, and I don't want to worry the family. I'm taking a break from the regimen. When we go to the mall tomorrow, I am going to eat whatever Oliver and Diane eat—no matter what. And when we have turkey on Thursday, I am helping Mom cook and am eating what is put on my plate. As much as I don't want to do it, this is my sacrifice for them.

12.13.95

Ugh, things are not going as planned. Thanksgiving was a bust. I couldn't bring myself to fulfill the resolution. I was so nervous about having to eat whatever Oliver and Diane ate while we were out shopping that I copped out and didn't even go. This means I still have to go Christmas shopping, but now when the malls are thronged with heavily cologned men desperately shopping for their wives and with little kids with runny noses running into you in the stuffy department stores.

Exams are stressing me out. Classes are a blur. I've looked at my notes so many times they're running together, which only makes me more nervous. Oliver yet again doesn't care what grades he makes, but thankfully Diane is as stressed out as I am. Laurie missed the last three days of school because of the flu. I've been blessed with a terrific immune system, which just goes to prove that Laurie and I are not in the same boat and she really was off base in comparing us. Oh well, when you're sick you don't see things clearly, I suppose.

The relatives begin to trickle in on Saturday, just in time to distract me from my math exam on Monday. The house is in a tumult because Mom is on her cleaning kick and there isn't a quiet spot anywhere to study.

However, all this worrying has proven somewhat useful—it certainly takes away the appetite.

12.25.95

Christmas Day and not a flake of snow outside; I guess it fits the mood. Holidays are usually a lot more exciting for me than this one has been. I mean, the relatives coming can be exhausting, but at least they provide entertainment. Plans fell through this year and only Pa and Grandma could come over. I hardly knew what to do without my younger cousins to baby-sit and my two older boy cousins pushing me around like I'm "one of the guys." I guess you can only miss them when they're gone.

My gifts bombed. I figured they would. If I had gone shopping with Oliver and Diane instead of waiting until the last minute when it was most crowded, I might have had a decent chance. But as it was, the gifts ended up being whatever I could snatch off displays and shove up to the counter to buy. Pa's was the only one I put real thought into. It was the best pocketknife I could find. He's not a big fan of all the "gizmos" as he calls them like miniscissors and a fingernail file, so I found him a navy blue-handled knife with a sturdy blade and screwdriver. I had his initials engraved on the side.

I bought it two months ago and have been dying to give it to him ever since. He cried a little when he opened it, as much from the gift as from the wrapping—I had wrapped it in a poem that took me longer to create than any I had written before. I had so much to say to him, and I wanted it to be perfect. I wanted him to know how much I love him, and words are my best expression.

Later in the day he whispered to me that he had never gotten a finer gift in his life, and I knew he meant the poem as much as the knife. I just said I was returning the favor and lifted this very journal. He smiled at me and winked.

MORGAN MENZIE

I helped Mom with the food, but it was harder than usual to get into it. Normally, we get up real early and make pigs-in-a-blanket (little smoked sausages wrapped in crescent rolls, for those of you who've never been deep-South enough to experience them), but this morning it was hard to roll out of bed—the fatty sausages and buttery crescent rolls only made me queasy. The big afternoon meal went the same way: lots of food that used to be appealing but now made me cringe. I ate it, of course, because I know Mom likes to hear how good the food tastes and see every one enjoying it. I think she likes that better than the food itself.

We have enough leftovers to last us until next Christmas. I don't think Mom and Grandma know how to cook for less than twenty even if there are only five of us there. The only good thing out of the whole day was that I was able to leave a little more on my plate than usual—portions can be deceiving when you get a little of everything and then only eat half of that little bit. It might be a good system if I learn how to develop it.

1996

1.2.96

One more year down. I am determined to have wonderful days for the next 365. I've decided I am skipping the awkward adolescent years. I will not be one of those people who looks at old pictures and grimaces while saying, *What was I thinking?!* Nope, I am going to be the first gracefully beautiful young adult.

I came to this conclusion over sparkling cider on New Year's Eve. Diane, Oliver and I had spent hours cutting construction paper to make confetti and watching some of my favorite movies that are a part of my everyday conversation which they cannot follow. We figured we would spend the long hours between dinner and midnight catching them up on my allusions so they could finally follow my train of thought.

We watched *When Harry Met Sally*. I think it is so romantic how fate kept drawing the two together until they had no choice but to fall in love.

I can be very mushy sometimes.

Oliver made "the gagging face" the entire time, but we ignored him. Diane and I decided that I should have Meg Ryan's hair because people always say I remind them of her. This is when I began to formulate the plan, and I don't plan to let myelf down.

Here's how it lines up:

1. *Lose weight! Lose weight! Lose weight!*

2. *Choose someone to look up to and study their habits, posture, and attitude until perfected (ie. Meg Ryan, Catherine from Wuthering Heights, or Lily Bart from The House of Mirth).*

3. *Do not succumb to the opposite sex until perfection is complete.*

4. Work out five times a week.

5. Cut out caffeine, carbonation, and try to stop fidgeting.

6. Get excellent grades. Graduate high school as valedictorian.

7. Develop a better dry wit.

8. Be nicer to parents.

9. Read one verse every night and write thoughts on it.

10. Pray.

2.14.96

Valentine's Day

Okay, enough is enough. Some ingenious middle school authority decided it would be fun to allow these puberty-ridden boys to purchase candy kisses for any secret crush they might desire. I quit! I've done my best not to watch Laurie like a hawk and pretend that the whole locker room episode never existed, and even Diane has commented on my progress. But this is just ridiculous! Laurie has received two whole bags of kisses—not that she's going to eat any of them. I, on the other hand, was delivered four kisses in a Ziploc bag. Three out of four were probably from my mother with the extra a kind gesture from Oliver. One of the four had crumbled from rough handling. It's a sign. My love life is doomed to a disastrous demise. You want to know the worst part? I ate them anyway.

I must hold myself more closely to the guidelines in the plan. The transformation has not begun to take effect, but once it does there is no stopping me. Forget Laurie; I'll beat her and her little kisses too. We'll see who gets more bags next year.
(Evil laugh.)

Note to self: Tomorrow, find a way to miss lunch.

3.5.96

Love is in the air! The crabapple trees are blooming all down my street, and the air smells sweeter. The days are brighter and the sky is bluer. I can't seem to keep myself from whistling when I'm outside—it's whistling weather. Everywhere I go people seem to be in a benevolent mood.

I uncharacteristically forgot one of my homework assignments (perhaps a side effect of spring, like kryptonite on Superman) and Mrs. Wilson didn't even skip a beat in offering an extension. Just when I had her pegged as a jaded middle-aged woman sapped of all human kindness, she surprises me!

Everyone's surprising me nowadays. For example, there's this guy, Owen, whom I had labeled as self-consumed and shallow—you know the type: pretty boy whose deepest concern is that his new Abercrombie hat is broken in enough to not look new. We were in the science lab yesterday, and in some horrible twist of fate he was assigned as my lab partner. I rolled my eyes, perhaps not so subtly, at the thought of doing the entire lab by myself. He caught the look and turned his attention on me, perhaps more fully than he has in all the years we have been at school together.

I was a bit ruffled by the look. I had been waiting for the cocky backlash, but what he turned on me was a look of curiosity that was unsettling. I had never noticed his brown eyes before, and they weren't half-bad. He proceeded to help all through the lab and tried to make conversation by asking me questions about my parents and Diane. I was too stunned by his sudden interest in my life that I don't even remember what I said—probably nothing more coherent than a mumbled reply.

I told Diane about the encounter after class, and she was quick to declare his love for me. She is convinced he has probably liked me for a while but never had the courage to pursue the thought. I said I had a hard time imagining him lacking the courage to do anything, but her insistence had awakened something in me. *Could I actually like someone of his social standing and attitude?* And if I did, how could he like someone like me: girl in not a lesser circle, but certainly in a different one, and who likes to talk to imaginary people in her journal?

Maybe it's because I'm losing weight.

3.25.96

It's spring break! I'm here in Florida with Diane and her family. It's a refreshing change; I usually go skiing in Colorado with my parents. I do like the cold weather better, but every now and then you need to shake things up. Plus, I feel like the cold weather has somehow gotten inside me this winter and never left. I am cold all the time.

We're in Destin where everyone from my school has been going since the beginning of time. I can't tell you how many times I have had to endure the spring break stories each year about the same people doing the same predictable things: falling in love, getting stung by a jellyfish, then getting "stung" by the new love. Even my teachers are here, which is odd because I've never thought of them as having any other life than that in the classroom. (Imagine your math teacher on the beach with her husband in a bathing suit. It blows the mind.)

The stories I've heard usually involved Owen. Normally this wouldn't interest me, but lately I've been noticing him more and more, and I wouldn't mind witnessing a few of these stories in action. Preferably him dumping whatever new girl he's with.

Of course, it's going to be rather difficult since I have sworn not to go out in public in a bathing suit. For starters, I think I am the only one here with a one-piece. Even Diane bought a modest two-piece. All the gorgeous girls at school, including Laurie, have gathered here in J. Crew and Victoria Secret bikinis. I don't stand a chance against any of them when it comes to Owen. We've already been here two days, and I've spent most of my time at the hotel pool watching Diane's siblings. Oliver has been trying to get me to come to the beach, but I've come up with an excuse both days.

I have a feeling it's only a matter of time.

MORGAN MENZIE

3.26.96

#3 on the list might as well be tossed out the window. I went to the beach today, but not before I'd gotten the courage to get Diane's mom to stop at the nearest mall so I could by a two-piece. If I was going to do this, I was going to do this right. I picked out a light blue bandeau top with white trimming and matching boy short bottoms. It was pretty cute and not so revealing that I felt naked, but I still felt extremely self-conscious and vowed to keep my T-shirt and shorts on the whole time.

Today was bright but very windy, and it was impossible to lie on the beach without being covered in sand, so most people went into the ocean. I, on the other hand, went to the beachside hut; bought a Diet Coke, which knocks #5 off the list; and sat on a stool to watch Diane play with her youngest sister, May. It was hot and the drink was cold, and I was feeling pretty happy and relaxed until someone tapped me on the shoulder.

It was Owen. I thought for sure he would be in the water with all the girls. He sidled up to me like a cowboy in a saloon. He was wearing red long surfer swim trunks and no shirt. My stomach fluttered, and then I got mad at myself for it.

"What are you doing way up here on the shore?"

"I was thirsty and thought I'd get something to drink."

"Are you still thirsty?"

"Well . . . no."

"Then let's go in the ocean. It's great out there. The waves are awesome."

"Oh, I don't know. I wasn't really planning to get in the water."

"Not planning to get in the water? Blythe, if you come to the beach, you have to get in the water."

"Well . . ."

Just then Oliver ran up.

"If you are trying to get her to go in the water, good luck, because I've been trying all week and it hasn't worked yet."

"Oliver, it's not that I don't want to get in the water. It's just . . ."

"Well, that settles it, you're coming in. Let's go, Oliver."

They both began to walk toward the water, and I had no choice but to follow them. I shot Diane a desperate look as I passed, my heart thumping as I jogged over the hot sand. I got to the edge and let the water rush up over my toes, hesitating at the prospect of taking off my T-shirt and shorts as they both dove in.

Owen, with a voice that sounded very far away, shouted up at me to come on in. Diane appeared by my side already in just her swimsuit and waited patiently for me to go in. Her presence was enough to give me the boost of courage I needed. The T-shirt came over my head, and I kicked the shorts off and got in the water up to my neck as quickly as possible. I was so thankful to be in the concealing water that I closed my eyes for a minute and let the wind whip my hair in front of my eyes.

Before I knew it, Owen was next to me gently tucking my hair behind my ear. Just as quickly he swam away saying, "By the way, that swimsuit looks great on you, Blythe."

I think I stopped breathing.

The rest of the day is a blur. If I weren't sunburned and there weren't still sand in my swimsuit, I wouldn't have believed it happened.

Yes, #3 is definitely off the list.

5.2.96

It's May and I feel the pressure of school. I have deliberately put Owen out of my mind in order to get through it. Exams are in two weeks and I have studied myself into a coma. It's affecting my vision—I'm having a hard time bringing things into focus even with my glasses, and if it weren't for my working out, I think my muscles would atrophy from the long hours bent over a desk.

I will do excellently on my finals. I must. Natural brainpower is not enough. I must push myself further until I accomplish my goals.

Mom is a little worried. I don't think I've spoken a whole sentence to her this whole month. I have to work on that, for that is not what I would call "being nicer to your parents." However I haven't spent very much time with anyone lately.

Poor Diane, I don't think she even remembers what I look like out from under the florescent school lights, and I haven't even *seen* Oliver in the past ten days. And Owen might as well be a figment of my imagination. But I know deep inside that this is why God gave me the gift of intelligence. He wants me to use it to its limits, to squeeze it dry of all its juices.

This will all pay off in the end. It must.

5.30.96

Summer

Do you ever wonder
Why people do what they do?
Why they trust who they trust?
Why they portray what they feel?
Do you ever wonder
Who really chooses the punishment?
Who executes the crime?
Who carries the guilt on her heart?
Do you ever wonder
If the world is coming to an end?
If your friends are really friends?
If you are as sane as you seem?
Do you ever wonder
What's hidden behind people's eyes?
What's the solution to the indefinable problem?
Or what you could have done differently if
you'd only had the chance?
Do you ever wonder
Why you stick with it?
Who plots with you and against you?
Or if now is a good time to just give up?
Do you ever wonder
What's the point in wondering?

MORGAN MENZIE

9.3.96

Eighth Grade—First Day
Weight: 107
Caloric intake: 800

Well, thus begins another monotonous year. As you can see I have implemented a new element to The Plan: recording weight and calories. Just think of it as a subsection to #1 on the list. This amendment will hopefully help me to measure my success more precisely so that I might make necessary adjustments to expedite the weight-loss method.

Sorry I haven't written in a while. I guess I've been preoccupied. Mom is starting to notice that I pick at my food—she's yet to notice the weight change, but I have a feeling it's only a matter of time. I've got to be more careful. It's a good thing we hardly ever eat together. I'd be caught for sure.

Oliver hasn't noticed, but Diane says she's worried about me. I tell her everything, so she knows what I've been doing. I can only hope her indecision on the matter will hold until I lose a few more pounds. The goal is 100. I can do it. I read the normal weight chart on the back of a pantyhose package—125 for 5'5"? They've gotta be kidding! Have they seen those Gap commercials? She's got to be six feet and 100 pounds at the most.

I've surpassed Laurie (thank you very much, no really, no applause, it was nothing). I think it was the summer that did it. It was so full of church camps and writing camps that I hardly had time to worry about food—it was easier to just skip meals entirely. Since our conversation in the locker room last fall, I've tried not to watch her in hopes that maybe if I don't, then she won't watch me. But I can't help but notice that I am smaller than she is. Now I'm glad I kept my promise not to tell, for she too is sworn to secrecy.

I look better in all my clothes than she does, and if she hadn't quit soccer I am sure I could confirm that my socks are lower than hers. Of course, it doesn't really matter that I've passed her, because she's leaving after this year to go to a different school. But it's at least nice to know that I've accomplished my goal.

Because of this success, I've set a new goal: Keep the family members and teachers in the dark. It's going to be tough, but isn't that what makes us grow?

Postscript: A new improvement has developed. Liz has finally left me alone. I think it had less to do with my now longer hair and more to do with my new personality. I've been so preoccupied with the diet that I don't have time for anything else—like worrying about what my peers think of me. Our strategic game of silence actually turned into indifference, and we've both gone our separate ways. I think she's finally got the picture that I don't care what she says. I've got my own goals to fulfill without added distractions. I think she's intimidated . . . checkmate.

MORGAN MENZIE

10.13.96

Weight: 103
Calories: 520

Just as summer comes and goes, romance dies. I can now admit with no embarrassment that I had a crush on Owen. I did not know it was a crush because I did not know he didn't feel the same way about me.

Diane, for all her kindness, is not a good judge of emotions. She just wanted him to like me as badly as I did, so she thought his feelings for me were more than they were. The worst part about it is that I convinced myself that Owen is a better person than he actually is. I gave him depth and maturity he does not deserve and may never achieve.

It happened Friday night at the football game. It was a big game . . . we were playing our rivals the Bobcats. I was as excited about it as much as anyone else, but not for the same reason: Owen had invited me to go to the game with him. Well, not exactly *with* him, but we were supposed to meet there.

It was especially cold that night, and I went shopping after school to get a really cute scarf. Mom dropped me off at the game early. Owen and I were supposed to meet at the brick entrance to the stadium and sit together. Normally I would have gone with Diane, but because it is so hard to round up her whole family, they normally show up toward the end of the first half. So I was all alone waiting. The wind was blowing straight through my jeans, and I hugged my coat tighter around me and waited. By the time the game had started my new scarf was over my ears and mouth and still no Owen. I was so busy shivering I didn't hear someone sneak up behind me.

"You know if the parking lot isn't what you were expecting, there's a football game going on in the other direction."

Thinking it was Owen and I had mixed up where we were supposed to meet, I turned with a big grin, but it was only Oliver. Despite the scarf practically hiding my face, he could see the disappointment in it.

"Hi."

"Don't sound so excited."

"I'm sorry, it's just that I was supposed to meet Owen here. I'm sure he's just running late."

"You mean *that* Owen?"

I looked where he was pointing, toward a distant lamppost. I was just in time to catch Owen and Liz walking hand in hand toward the stadium encircled in light. Something dropped in the pit of my stomach, and I stopped shivering from sheer shock.

Liz had won after all.

"Come on, Blythe. Let's go watch the game."

Oliver was tugging me toward the glaring lights of the field. Although I had no interest in the game, I let him lead me in and sit me down in the midst of warm bodies. He left me there in a daze, and by the time he returned with hot chocolate, which I already knew I wasn't going to drink, I was engrossed in Owen and Liz cuddling. My life was finally like a movie, but instead of a great romantic comedy, I was a made-for-TV teen drama.

They had sat down right in front of me. He was rubbing her shoulders like he should have been rubbing mine. Oliver shoved the steaming Styrofoam cup under my nose and, unthinking, I took a big gulp, hoping it would ease the pain. Quickly realizing what I had done, I spit it out in the cup or at least *aimed* for the cup. The spray was too forceful, and I overshot it and hit Liz with a shower of warm liquid down her neck. She squealed and the hysterics began. Before I had realized what I had done, Oliver had taken the cup from me and was now apologizing to Liz.

"So sorry, Liz, I didn't think it was going to be that hot. Burned my tongue actually. You understand though. I'm sure you've been burned by something before."

Liz had stopped shouting and was now glaring suspiciously at me and Oliver.

"You clumsy idiot! That is so gross. It's something I would have suspected from Blythe, not you!"

"Once again, I am very sorry. Would you like the rest of my hot chocolate? It's sure to warm you up."

Before I knew what I was doing I burst out laughing and Owen, who had seen the whole thing and knew I was the culprit, stifled a laugh and started to pat Liz with napkins. He was trying to console her when Oliver pulled me away.

"What was that about?"

"What? Oh that. Like you said, it was hot."

He gave me a skeptical look, but I kept a straight face. How could I explain that one sip of hot chocolate could have ruined my eating record? He just looked at me for a few more seconds and then turned away saying, "Well watch out. Next time I might not be able to save you."

11.25.96

Weight: 111 (so close!)
Calories: 400

I escaped Thanksgiving this year! There's something to be thankful for! I'm spending the holiday with Diane and Oliver with his family at their lake house. It took a lot of maneuvering on my part; Mom and Dad don't think I'm spending enough time at home. I told them that since none of the relatives are coming until Christmas, I could go to the lake now and spend lots of time with the family later.

We went fishing on the partially frozen lake. It was cold, but fun. I made Oliver bait all my hooks, and Diane and I took turns with the extra pole. I've never laughed so much in my entire life. Oliver's parents were busy at the house preparing for this afternoon's meal, and his brother was driving up from college and wasn't there yet. It was just Diane, Oliver, and me on the lake.

First of all, Diane was afraid of all the things in the water she couldn't see, and Oliver and I both kept rocking the boat to scare her until we did almost tip over. It was just a rowboat, so when we were rocking it we accidentally dropped one of the oars in the water and all had to steer with our hands to catch up with the drifting oar.

Once Oliver caught a fish, and I was supposed to dip the net in the water to get it out but just as I had almost gotten it, it jerked free from the hook and went crazy. The minute its slimy back touched me I yelped, dropped the net, and wiped my hand on the closest thing I could find: Oliver's coat. He would not stop making fun of me. He said I wouldn't last one day in the woods. I said I would too if everything slimy stayed away from me. We came back with no bait, no net, and no fish.

It was great.

MORGAN MENZIE

The meal wasn't that bad either. Everyone was so busy talking at once and listening to Oliver's brother tell about college that no one paid any attention to what anybody ate or didn't eat. It wasn't at all like my Thanksgivings at home. It was much better. It was loud and disorderly and filled with laughter. I felt relaxed and calm and thankful for the hunger that was able to stay put in my stomach all through the meal.

I wish my life were full of these moments, but I guess the rarity of it makes it all the better.

12.6.96

Weight: 101 (constancy, ugh)
Calories: 400

This is the worst part of the year. I've just gotten back from Thanksgiving break, and Christmas is right around the corner. The last thing I want to do is schoolwork. I know I've vowed to pursue academic excellence with a fervor, but I just can't seem to concentrate. In a desperate attempt to awaken the scholar in me, I watched *Dead Poet's Society* for the five-hundredth time. It usually does the trick. By the time I'm rewinding, not only am I ready to study, I am also willing to challenge all the men and women that have gone before me in the greatness of my own unique path. But it didn't help this time. It just wasted two hours and made me wish I had Robin Williams as a teacher. Exams are looming, and I'm without a single drop of motivation.

I told Oliver this, foolishly thinking he would sympathize and help turn my thoughts to academia. Oh, how I misjudged him. He just laughed at me and told me to stop worrying (as if that is possible). He convinced me that what I needed was fresh air. He said I had been trapped in the house and the academy too long. My brain was tired, he said, of swimming in stale air. He promised that if I went on a walk with him, studying would soon come as easy as breathing. So I went.

It is beautiful out on his parents' land. The earth stretches out behind his house in a gentle slope so that you can see for miles around. The day was crisp and the sky was so blue you wanted to touch it. We walked down a winding path, past this field and into the forest that lay beyond. I felt as if I were an adventurer setting out on a long road ahead. I began to imagine what sorts of things would meet me around every bend.

Oliver and I didn't talk much at first. We just walked, listening to the leaves crunch under our feet. Without even realizing when the conversation started or who initiated it, we found ourselves in the mist of talking about school and the future, and I had started to tell him the story I had worked up in my head about the forest in which we walked—making it up as we went along.

If we emerged into a clearing, it was the very spot on which only moments ago the fallen knight had lain to rest—dreaming away his troubles while staring up at the sky. When we crossed a little stream, it was the fountain of youth for which many had quested and died in vain.

I continued with encouraging laughs or comments from Oliver until the path ended at a cliff overlooking the valley and hills of the surrounding countryside. You could feel the spaciousness in the air. All of a sudden I wasn't worried about school or eating or family holidays. I was just here. I had stopped talking and a sigh of contentment escaped.

Oliver said in a hushed and reverent voice, "Didn't I tell you this was exactly what you needed?"

12.26.96

Christmas Break
Weight: 100
Calories: 400

Woohoo! The Plan is working! I've finally reached the goal and passed with flying colors. And they say you gain weight over the holidays. Ha! It's strange though, I'm not quite satisfied yet . . . just a little more, and it'll be right as rain. You can tell the relatives are here—I'm talking like Grandma—*right as rain*.

Speaking of Grandma, she didn't say her usual refrain this year: "Why Blythe! You're as cute as a speckled pup under a red wagon!" And before you ask, I have no idea what it means. Anyway, instead she just looked at me and said, "Darlin', why don't I fix you a nice plate of sausage and biscuits like I used to."

Never before in my life have I been so panicked. I know it's just Grandma. She's not exactly the most intimidating creature around. If you think about it, she's getting shorter by the second; but still, my heart skipped a beat. I politely said, "No thank you," and that I had already eaten, but she looked at me with those all-knowing Grandma eyes and asked, "Where's your mother?"

I don't know why I didn't want to tell her. I don't know why I felt like a criminal about to be ratted out, but I pointed toward the kitchen and scurried out of the house like a jackrabbit on the run. Nothing ever came of it though. I made it through the meal, cringing at each bite and wishing I were at Oliver's lake house. I felt like all the eyes around the table were on me, but I didn't look up even once. I could feel Grandma next to me, her staring eyes and her worried breathing. I hate it that I can't even be myself around Grandma anymore.

MORGAN MENZIE

Oh well, we all make sacrifices.

School starts back up in a few days, and I'll be back to the old routine. Christmas disrupted my whole regimen. It's a miracle I was able to keep the weight down. I've never been so ready to get out from under the family's watchful eye in my life!

1997

1.1.97

Happy New Year! In case you're wondering why I didn't weigh myself, it is because I figure if the days run together with no sleep in between then it counts as one big, long day—hence the weight from the thirty-first carries over to the first.

Diane and I finally finished watching *Sleepless in Seattle* this year. We fell asleep halfway through it last December. And Oliver came and didn't make fun of it at all. In fact, he was pretty quiet all night. When the ball finally fell he cheered up a little, and we all toasted with sparkling cider and hugged and threw streamers.

I watched the movie through new eyes tonight. What caught my attention this time was the *Affair to Remember* subplot. That's what I want! I want a man to shake me out of my comfort zone and bring to life everything in me that I thought was dormant or never existed. Owen could not do this. So there must be someone else out there who can. I want him to pine for me and paint pictures of me and never love anyone else but me. I know this is a lot to ask, but isn't that what love is: a lot to ask?

Carrying over from last New Year, I have revised my list:

1. Lose weight (as always)!
2. Learn to rely on myself.
3. If falling in love is inevitable, do not get heartbroken; he should be the one to put his heart on the line.
4. Working out builds muscle which weighs more than fat, so if I must, only do aerobic exercise.
5. Caffeine is not the enemy! Embrace it!
6. Do not slack in school.

7. Get closer to my friends—they will stick by me in the end.

8. Laugh as much as possible for it cheers you up and burns lots of calories.

1.7.97

Weight: blah
Caloric intake: blah (Blame it on the holidays.)

It's a dreary day, and my mood seems to be in the same state. Of course, it doesn't help that I haven't lost any weight in a whole two weeks! One hundred pounds is such a ridiculously static number. When I'm around my friends I paste on a happy front (I've begun to avoid Diane and Oliver—it's too hard to lie to them, and they worry about me enough as it is).

Occasionally when attention is drawn to me, I make a funny comment, smile wryly and hope to be left in peace, if you could call this peace. It seems these days the only way to express my feelings is to write them. This journal has become my only solitude. When all else seems to fall apart around me, I still have this on which to cling. These pages are a balm to my soul. For if I speak up and say what I am feeling, I am sure to get criticized as sounding too morose and not like my normal self. These bound pages come without criticism.

Nobody truly knows me, but I suppose that's the way it is for everyone. Or at least I hope so. We seem to have the tendency to put on a front in the best interest of ourselves, but eventually these fronts weld themselves to us until we no longer recognize our own soul in the mirror.

The Fantasy:

It just thundered. A storm's coming. I adore storms. I often dream of moving to Scotland where there is a constant mist and a gentle fog rolling over the moorlands. I would go off to boarding school so I could be on my own. It would be in an elegant castle with polished wooden floors and walls made of the most beautiful ancient stone. Moss should grow on the rooftop and vines climb up the turrets—there must be turrets. We would all wear straight gray jumpers and Mary Janes and ribbons in our hair.

It would be a place where a poet could be inspired and never lose her "deepness." The words would flow on paper like leaves in a brook during autumn. The scenery would never be less than picturesque. It would fill me with all the characteristics that I have been searching for to perfect myself. I would come home with a wisdom and maturity that could only be cultivated in a place like Scotland. I would be wise in the ways of the world.

I know even as I write this there may never be such a place, but if I am to be stuck here, I must have one escape to the paradise in my thoughts.

Diane hates it when I talk like this. She says it scares her. She says she hardly knows me anymore. She doesn't understand. She has a house full of sisters to keep her busy. I am all alone with the parents. She has never known loneliness.

I think we're drifting apart. She's drifting toward the enveloping arms of her family and God. I'm drifting toward the rocky shore of nothingness. Fitzgerald was right, "So we beat on, boats against the current, borne back ceaselessly into the past."

Oh well, it's probably better this way. I'm not good for anyone right now.

MORGAN MENZIE

2.14.97

Valentine's Day!

Kisses, kisses everywhere and not a bite to eat! I now have proof that The Plan has worked to my full advantage. Today is "The Day of the Kisses." Today hearts are made and broken. And today I received more than I dared to dream.

During third period the passing out of the kisses begins. Names are in alphabetical order, so I know I am near the front. The anticipation is huge. I feel that my plan hinges on the outcome of this event. Then I hear "Beaumont, Blythe" and I can't think anymore! I just walk to the front, collect my bags and sit back down, not looking.

Eventually I hear Diane's voice cut through the daze, "Holy cow, Blythe! You got a million kisses. Somebody sure loves you. Who do you think they're from?"

I finally looked down—not only were there kisses, which cost ten cents each, but there were also hugs, which cost fifteen cents a piece! Five brimming bags of love sat on my desk. And can you believe it—my first feeling was frustration. I couldn't enjoy them because I did not know who sent them. The idea was to leave it at anonymous adoration, but I never liked suspense. I had to find out who sent them.

I spent the lunch hour asking everyone I knew if they had sent me the kisses; by now it had gotten around that I had received more than the normal share. Diane admitted she sent me four, which I had assumed because I had sent her four also, but other than her, no one took the credit. I decided to interrogate Oliver because if he didn't do it himself, being a male, he would know who did.

"Oliver did you send me those kisses?"

"Now Blythe, what's the fun in it if you know who sent them?"

"It's not funny, so stop smiling. I can't enjoy them if I don't know who sent them."

"You should just be grateful for them."

"Don't preach at me. And stop laughing!"

"It's just funny to see you so worked up over this. Just when I think I have you figured out, you surprise me."

I refused to let him sidetrack me.

"Well, if you didn't send them, then who did?"

"Well I . . ."

Just then Owen runs up behind me and grabs my waist. I was so surprised I forgot to be self-conscious.

"Thought you might like something special on Valentine's Day."

Then he kissed me on the cheek, smiled a slow smile, and ran off.

I stood there speechless.

Finally I realized Oliver was staring at me, so I whispered, still looking after him, "I guess we know who sent the kisses."

3.3.97

Weight: 95
Calories: 300
Day: Horrible, miserable, never want to experience again

Everyone is out to get me. Today started out so great, and then it all fell down the rabbit hole. I woke up this morning and began my regular routine: go to the bathroom, strip down, and weigh myself. Glory be, I had finally reached my new and improved goal: 95 pounds. Isn't that just a wonderfully fragile number—I was meant to be in the double digits. I was in such a good mood that I woke up the house whistling to myself.

Side note: I have an unusually loud whistle. It appears God had compensated for my lack of vocal talent by endowing me with the best airflow in the Western Hemisphere.

Anyway, the whistling startled Mom, who is a light sleeper. She came down the hall like a cat on fire. I was just heading out for my morning jaunt to the gym, and it was still dark out. I didn't see Mom when she cornered the hallway. We collided at the back door. Here's how the conversation unfolded:

"Blythe, we have to talk."

"What, Mom! You scared me to death! I gotta go or I'm never going to be able to work out before school."

"Why do you need to work out at five o'clock in the morning? It's not healthy the way you never slow down."

"Mom, do we really have to get into this right now? I've already explained to you that I have too much work to do after school to afford any time to exercise then. Besides, I like to go ahead and get it done. What do you mean, 'not healthy'?"

"Sit down, Blythe."

This is the point at which Mom began to cry. Oddly enough, all I could think of was how the gray light of dawn made her look very, very old. All of a sudden I began to cry, too. I needed her, and she looked so old and sad. It scared me.

"I've been talking with your teachers, and they've made me face something I was not ready to see."

"Mom, I really have to go."

"No, no you don't, and I don't think you should be exercising today."

Panic struck me like a splash of icy water. Anger overcame my tears.

"Mom, what are you talking about! You're freaking me out, and I don't have time for this. I have to go."

Mom became a lot less fragile.

"Sit down! I know you're not eating, and I see how you work out excessively. If you think I haven't noticed how much weight you've lost, you're wrong."

This stopped me dead in my tracks.

"I don't know what you're talking about."

"Blythe, your teachers have noticed and even your grandmother said something. I don't know what to do. I don't know what has made you do this, but your father and I have been talking, and we think you need to get some help."

"I *don't* need help! And I do too eat, so just back off!"

Before I knew it I was crying uncontrollably. In between sobs I managed to mumble, "It's all Laurie's fault anyway."

"What? What are you talking about? Blythe, honey, look at me."

"Never mind. It's nothing."

"One of your teachers knows of a nice nutritionist who has helped girls get through this in the past. She's a Christian, and I have talked to her. She seems genuine. I think you should give her a try."

MORGAN MENZIE

Something in me crumbled. It was as if my fortress of cards fell apart with one burst of breath, and I was left exposed grasping at air. It was like a taut rubber band supporting the Brooklyn Bridge had snapped, and I tumbled into the murky water. Mom just held me and hugged me. We were both crying and all she said was, "You're still my little girl, Blythe, and I'll always love you. You're still my little girl."

I went through the day with my face swollen from crying and a sullen attitude. I was going to be strong about this. As soon as the initial breaking had passed, my determination and resentment kicked back in. No one would make me stop the only thing that made me happy in the last year. Of course, the minute I saw Diane and she looked at me with knowing eyes, I broke down again.

During lunch we sat outside on the concrete steps that had become our refuge. It was where we could be as we were: best friends without any complications, if only for an hour. She hugged me and said that she'd be praying for me. Oddly enough, that hit me like a dead weight. I realized that I had no faith that her prayers would make any difference. I just nodded and mumbled a thank you. God could do no more for me than Diane could. It was a sharp reminder of how far the two of us had drifted. Not even the steps could bring us back together.

Suddenly I needed Oliver. I needed him to make me laugh like he always does so that I could forget about all this.

3.5.97

Weight: Not allowed to weigh
Calories: Not allowed to count

Week One of Nutritional Chemotherapy

"I'm in high school! Do I really need my mom to pack my lunch for me?!"

This was the first thing I said to Rebecca Barton who prefers "just Becca." At first I thought it wasn't going to be so bad; you know, go in, talk about food and nutritional content (I've got that down pat) and then leave. I was so wrong. Becca No-Last-Name is located downtown in a crowded seventies-style building that smells like old cigarettes and car fresheners. Both Mom and Dad drove me down there—talk about awkward. Mom's trying to make small talk and not sound nervous in the car as Dad takes every curve like it's the Daytona 500. He always drives fast and a little too crazy, but I think it was especially bad today. I think he was nervous.

When we finally got there, all three of us had to sit in this tiny waiting room. It was too hot in there, and the walls were painted a rather blinding yellow. It was probably a psychological ploy to soothe, but all it did was make me have to go to the bathroom.

When Becca took us in her office, I had to sit in this stuffy leather chair that looked like it came out of Batman's parlor while Mom and Dad sat on the couch a little behind me. I couldn't see them because of the winged sides of the Batman chair that stuck out like blinders.

Because of this visual blockage, it made everything they said sound more ominous. They could have sung "Somewhere over the Rainbow" and it would have sounded like a funeral dirge. Becca seemed overly cheerful toward them and overly serious toward me. It was like watching the theater masks being put on and pulled off. Pretty soon she got going so fast I thought her face would get stuck in some twisted grimace with twinkling eyes.

Becca told my parents that we were going to "nip this thing in the bud." When the conversation lulled, I kept wondering what bud she could be talking about. She seemed too young to be a professional anything. She could have been my age! The thing that snapped me back to attention was Dad's frustrated words to Becca, whom he refused to call anything but Ms. Barton. In a burst of impotent anger he gritted, "I am not going to let her die!"

Die, I thought, *who said anything about dying*? I had to hold back a nervous laugh. I didn't want to look at him even if I could have. I desperately wanted to sink into the polished leather until I was just part of the false glaze.

When my parents were excused, Becca left the serious face on for good. She has an eerie way of looking too closely into my eyes. I felt like she was trying to stare right through my head. *If she pulls out the Bible and makes me kneel, I'm running for the door*, I thought.

Instead, she asked, "When did you stop eating?"

To which I replied, "I haven't stopped," and looked at the floor.

She never lost the stare and began again, "When did you start restricting?" When I looked at her with a question in my eyes, she elaborated, "When did you stop letting yourself eat what you wanted to eat?"

I thought for a minute and replied, "Beginning of last year, I guess. But I haven't stopped eating."

She wrote something down in her chart.

"How often do you think about food during the span of one day?"

I politely told her I had no idea.

She began to throw out numbers, "25 percent, 40 percent, 70 percent?"

I thought for a moment and said quietly, "85."

After that it was less questions and more instructions. She made me get on her scale backward, so I wouldn't see my weight. I couldn't help thinking that this isn't fair because it's the middle of the day and I have all my clothes on, which is not how I usually weigh myself. There were too many variables in her system.

Mental note: wear lighter clothes next time.

She handed me a chart of what she called minimums. It was a list of all the different amounts of grains and fruits and dairy and the dreaded fats that I was supposed to get in a day.

I took one look at the list and said, "There's no way I can do this," to which Becca referred to the charts as a goal to work up to.

She couldn't help adding that, "Ideally you are supposed to get to a point where you eat above the minimums, because they are still considered restricting."

She's a real peach, I thought to myself, but just smiled and nodded. With that one sentence, she crossed over to my bad side.

She also gave me little folded pamphlets that looked like brochures. Each fold was divided into four sections: breakfast, lunch, dinner, and snack. I was supposed to write what I had eaten and how many servings so that she and I could keep track of my minimums. There was a section at the bottom called the "exercise log," and I politely asked how much I could work out. To my astonishment she said, "None at all until you get your weight up." I wanted to throw all her pamphlets and charts in her face, but instead I just smiled and nodded.

This is going to be tricky.

There was no small talk in the car on the way home. All three of us had enough to think about. But I couldn't help studying the expressions on their faces and trying to guess what they were thinking.

MORGAN MENZIE

First step: Put Mom's and Dad's minds at ease. No use in worrying over nothing. I've always been the good daughter and I will
be again, even if it takes sweet-talking until the end of eternity.
   Ugh.

3.9.97

The Beginning of the Chart

Breakfast:
Cereal (1 serving, grain)
Milk (2 servings, dairy)
Grapes (1 serving, fruit)

Lunch:
Turkey sandwich with lettuce (2 servings, protein;
    2 servings, grain; 1 serving, veggie)
Honey mustard pretzels (2 servings, grain)
Apple (1 serving, fruit)

Dinner:
Sushi—crab, shrimp, cucumber, rice (2 servings,
    protein; 2 servings, grain)
Honey mustard pretzels (2 servings, grain)

Snacks:
Mixed nuts (2 servings, protein)

I wonder if they'll notice that I embellished just a tad? Who cares? They can make me do this, but they can't make me tell the truth. My first and foremost goal is to settle my parents' worries. Everything else takes second place. So, Becca-no-last-name, here's my list, take it or leave it. See if I care.

If I could be where I wished,
Whenever that wish occurred to me,
I'd rarely ever be seen.
For if I could, I'd set myself free,
Free to disappear and just watch,
As the actors step on stage,
And with every glance a turn of the page,
In the book of my life,
Which I'd write for myself.
To write a wish,
A wish to go unseen,
For that would set me free.

4.17.97

Breakfast:
Cereal (2 servings, grain)
Skim milk (2 servings, dairy)

Lunch:
Turkey on wheat (2 servings, protein; 2 servings grain)
Lowfat potato Salad (1 serving, dairy; 1 serving, protein)

Dinner:
Baked Chicken (2 servings, protein)
Green beans (2 servings, vegetable)
Yeast roll (1 serving, grain)

Ugh, Christian academy life is not all it's cracked up to be. News must have gotten around that I'm seeing a nutritionist. How, I don't know. The only people who knew were the teachers who recommended Becca, and they're supposed to be above the fray aren't they? It's odd how the information leaked from such impervious creatures as teachers.

Every day at least a dozen well-meaning, good Christian peers come up to me, place their hand on my shoulder, stare deeply into my eyes and ask, "How are you doing?"

Shall I translate? "Tell me what's happening to you so I can tell all my friends."

It amazes me how much people seem to change and "genuinely" care when you're having a really scandalous problem. I could be quietly suffering for years and not one glance could turn my way. But let a little drama leak out and everyone is ready to lay hands on me.

To make matters worse, Laurie and Liz seemed to have teamed up against me. Liz has taken this as her chance to get back at me for the hot chocolate incident. And I suppose that Laurie has decided to use this as her last hurrah before she leaves for good. She has decided she's too good for us here at the Academy. She's off to boarding school somewhere up in New England. I have a feeling it's more about both her parent's new relationships than it is about higher education. Anyway, she and Liz have suddenly become fast friends. I see them whispering when I walk down the hall. And I see them staring at me in class. All this I could handle if they had just kept their distance, but yesterday they approached me in the lunch line.

"We heard you were having some trouble lately, Blythe. How are you?"

"Oh, I'm fine thanks."

"No really. How are you? Is there anything we can do?"

"Do about what?"

"Oh, you know, anything."

"Well, I'm great. Is there anything I can do for you?"

"No, no we're great, too. Is there anything you want us to pray for?" As she said this, Laurie slipped me a neatly-folded note.

"Well, actually . . . I'm having some trouble at school."

"Oh really—trouble how?"

"Well, there seems to be these two girls who have never been particularly nice to me, and now all of a sudden they want to jump into my life. I feel like they're sticking their noses where they don't belong. Could you pray that God may grant me patience and that He will give these girls much-needed wisdom?"

I don't know what made me say it. I shouldn't have. It only made things worse, but the words just came out. I couldn't stop them. I turned around to walk out of the room and found myself face to face with Owen. He was laughing uncontrollably and pointing at Laurie and Liz. I just smiled wryly and walked on, leaving the girls slack-jawed and Owen laughing at them.

It felt bad. It felt wonderfully bad.

Of course, Oliver and Diane didn't think it was very funny, but I didn't see them stick up for me either, so they can't talk.

5.30.97

Memorial Day

Breakfast:
Toast with butter (2 servings, grain; 1 serving, fat)

Lunch:
Cereal (2 servings, grain)
Milk (2 servings, dairy)
Banana (1 serving, fruit)

Dinner:
Turkey hot dog (1 serving, protein)
Wheat bun (2 servings, grain)
Low-fat potato salad (2 servings, grain;
   2 servings, protein; 1 serving, fat)
Angel food cake (1 serving, with strawberries;
   2 servings, fruit)

Snack:
Blueberry snow cone (2 servings, of nothing but sugar)

Okay—I hate holidays! It's worse now that I'm seeing Becca because everyone in my entire family watches what I eat. They try to be sly about it, but I see them looking. I've jumped at Mom for it so many times that she's afraid to say anything to me at all. I was doing so well today, too. I had managed to lie in bed long enough this morning to miss the huge family breakfast. And when lunch came, I ate earlier than everyone else so I could eat or not eat what I wanted. It was dinner that got me.

It must have been 500 degrees outside, but some bright

individual, who I am ashamed to say is a relative, decided we ought to grill out. It was the most stressful ordeal I've been through as of yet.

Grandma pulled me aside and looked me up and down. Trying to be cheerful she said, "Well, my girl, looks like we've got to get some meat on those bones."

I didn't say anything. The image was too crude. I pictured myself being tied down while all my relatives pasted strips of raw meat to me like papier-mâché. The thoughts must have registered to a horrific look on my face because Grandma quickly said, "Now, now, Blythe, are you feelin' okay? You look a little pale. Should I get your mother?" I just shook my head and walked away. Only two more hours until I could escape to Diane's and watch the fireworks.

The grilling commenced, and I secretly slipped a turkey dog on the fire. I stared anxiously at the criss-cross patterns the flipped dogs made, trying to keep my eye on the one with half the calories. It was like trying to keep your eye on the queen in a card game. I was never very good at cards—too competitive. At one point Mom tried to pull me away to take a family picture, but I demanded to be left to tend the food and volunteered Dad, the chef, to join the photo shoot. She gave me a sad look, but I didn't care if it meant I was free to baby-sit my food.

I wasn't up to being in a picture anyway—not while I was imagining myself stuffed and fat after eating that grotesque meat. I just knew the grease from the artery-cloggers was getting on my turkey dog.

After the meal, Mom took me to Diane's, and I jumped out of the car before she could give me any kind of talk. I think I'm growing paranoid. Once in the presence of my best friend I felt a little better. I put the whole dinner episode behind me and helped hold sparklers for her four sisters. The youngest, May, was a little afraid of the bright sparks, but I sat with her in the grass and held it at arm's length until she grew brave enough to put her little hand on top of mine while we wrote her name in the sky with light.

By the end of the night when the firecrackers had run out, I smelled of gunpowder smoke and had a garland of daisies around my neck that May and I had created. Diane and I lay in the grass and absently searched for four-leaf clovers. I told her about the dinner and how it was so strange to be so freaked and stressed out by it. I told her I didn't know what to do, and I began to cry a little. Like always, she hugged me and said she'd pray for me. I didn't feel quite as big a resentment as usual. I figured Diane would have a better in with God than I would, so it couldn't hurt if she talked to Him for me. I'll take all the help I can get.

All in all it ended up being a good night. We slept in her basement where it was cool on the pullout couch like we had so many times before. I think Diane is the only person I feel safe with right now. Of course I also know she won't challenge me. It's not in her nature to seek out conflict.

6.1.97

Weight: 103
Caloric Intake: 100

I can't believe I've gained three pounds! This is ridiculous. It's probably because of that stupid turkey hot dog. That's it; I'm giving up everything that isn't fruit, vegetable, or water. I wasn't supposed to see the number, but I cheated and looked while Becca was writing it down. She was so proud. She just kept saying what progress I've made and how the food charts look promising. I wonder if she knows I fudged a little? I bet not.

Well, it's time for a makeover of sorts. The calories have to come down and the food charts had better beef up. That's another one of Grandma's phrases—beef up. Ugh, it has such a gross connotation. I feel like I need to brush my teeth afterward.

I'm not supposed to be weighing myself, but I sneaked the scale out of the attic and hid it in my bathroom under the sink, under towels. Why should Becca get to see and not me? This is one of the things that I haven't told Diane. I used to think it was impossible to tell her a lie, but now it's just easier for both of us if she doesn't know. She doesn't know how serious everyone else thinks my disease is. Don't you just love how they call it a "disease"? It sounds so foreboding, as if it came straight out of Edgar Allen Poe's basement. I like referring to *my disease*. It gives my life a little drama. (If God won't help me out with some happiness now and then, I've got to find some on my own.)

Back to Diane. I told her that I'm getting much better and that Becca thinks I'm making huge progress—which is not a lie. She did say I was *making big steps*. Diane feels better when my life is rosy. She worries so much about me, and it makes me sad to think of her worrying. I don't need any more sadness in my life at the moment.

MORGAN MENZIE

I told her to keep praying, that I could use a little divine inter-vention. I figure if I've got someone with connections, I might as well use her. I don't say the word "disease" around her. I just say "my issue."

"I really am getting over my issue. It's hardly a problem any-more."

I see the relief in her eyes, and it gives me some peace. I wonder if she's noticed the three pounds of lard that have latched themselves to my once-thin frame? Probably not, and that's what I'm counting on. If she doesn't notice me gain weight, she won't notice me lose it either.

6.5.97

Weight: 102
Calorie intake: 250

Okay, I'm a little worried about my deceiving Diane. Why can I lie so easily to everyone else, but when it comes to her, I'm a big glob of guilt? It's not that I really lie to Mom or Dad or Becca; it's just that I don't want to cause any trouble. In the end they like it better that way, too. Maybe it's because Diane trusts me so much. The unquestioning trust that I'm "getting better" gets me every time. It's that best-friend mentality.

I talked to her on the phone not two minutes ago. She wanted me to come over and watch a movie with her family. Her dad was going to make his old-fashioned popcorn on the stove. She said I could pick the movie. I said I had summer reading to do. It's true. I do have summer reading. It's just not imperative that I do it right this minute. But of course, being the compassionate friend that she is, she just said, "Oh, I understand totally. I should be doing my reading, too. Oh well, you're just more disciplined than me. I love ya, and I'll talk to ya soon."

I could feel the knife twisting in my heart. But I mumbled, "I love you too," and hung up the phone.

I just need a tougher skin is all. I should be able to pull this off. It'll just take some determination and sacrifice. And it will be better for both of us when I lose this awful fat. I'll be a happier person when I feel good about myself again. It's really all Becca's fault for making me do something I don't want to do. She's forcing me to lie to everyone I love.

7.12.97

Weight: 101

Mentality: *depressed, depressed, depressed*

I almost blacked out today when Mom and I were sitting in the waiting room before I saw Becca. I stood up to get a magazine and everything went dark. It was like a movie fade out, only I didn't enjoy it. I had to keep blinking really fast and fanning myself until my vision cleared. I don't think Mom noticed. She was reading an article in *Southern Living* on how to keep your flowers looking fresh all year long. I sat back down and shut my eyes real tight and began to pray. I know, I know—what happened to all my healthy agnosticism and Christian school rebellion? The thing is, I panicked and my first thought was to pray. I guess I'm a bit of a hypocrite.

> Dear Lord,
>   Please help me to get better. Please don't ever let me feel that terrible again. I'm sorry I haven't prayed lately, and I'm sorry I haven't been listening to You. Please take care of me and let me rest in You. I want to be well for You. I need Your help, because I can't do this without You . . . .

Before I knew it, I felt less like a hypocrite and more like a Christian. Oddly enough I was not surprised at this. All I could think of as I prayed was that I want to feel this kind of peace forever. I went on praying like this until it was my time to go in to see Becca. I didn't tell her what had happened. When I got home I found this verse:

my whole being, praise the LORD
    and do not forget all his kindnesses.
He forgives all my sins
    and heals all my diseases.
He saves my life from the grave
    and loads me with love and mercy.
He satisfies me with good things
    and makes me young again, like the eagle.

PSALM 103:2-5

See, it's a sign. God is telling me that He will fix everything. He's telling me that He will forget all the stupid stuff I've done, and He will give me my innocence back. I knew it all along. Now maybe God loves me as much as Diane. All I had to do was ask Him.

7.18.97

Breakfast:
milk (2 servings, dairy)
Oatmeal (1 serving, grain)
Orange (1 serving, fruit)

Lunch:
Subway turkey on wheat with lettuce, onions,
   jalapenos (2 servings, protein; 2 servings,
   veggies; 2 servings, grain)
Sunchips (2 servings, grain)
Peach yogurt (2 servings, dairy)

Dinner:
Veggie Stew with beef and potatoes, green beans,
   okra, corn, carrots: (3 servings, veggies;
   2 servings, protein; 2 servings, starch)
Corn bread (2 servings, grain)

Snack:
mint chocolate chip ice cream (2 servings, dairy)

I'm starting school soon. Just a week and I'll be in high school.
I've been working with Becca for two months, and I've gained
about eight pounds. I think that merits a review of my records
and special consideration for parole. I've been getting my minimums down, and Mom says I'm much happier now. I think I
agree, and I know why: I found a better way to get all my food
in the day, and it's much more fun. I eat just a little throughout
the day and then when night comes I get to eat whatever I want.

It's sort of a treat for making it through the day. It gives me something to look forward to. I enjoy food now instead of running away from it. It's fun to think of all the foods I can eat when I get home. And there's no guilt involved because everyone is telling me to gain weight.

My plan is to gain two more pounds before school starts and proceed to work my way out from under Becca's grasp. Dad even said he thinks I might be out of the hole.

Diane is much more inclined to hang out with me now that I'm happier. We act crazy together, and next week we're going school-supply shopping. Surround me with office supplies and I'm like a kid in a candy store. I've convinced her to take Latin with me. It's about time I put my brain to good use. Gets my mind off rehab.

The thing that keeps nagging me though is that I'm not all that much happier than I was before. I know everybody thinks I am, but the minute I get alone it just hits me like a wave. The world gets smaller and darker all around me. Sure I have more energy to pretend like I'm cool, but I don't really feel genuinely better. If this is the way it feels to be normal, I'd almost rather be thin and less happy.

I know this doesn't really make sense, but I guess I don't think it should be such a big issue what I weigh. Becca's always telling me that it's not the number that counts. If that's true, why is it that the only way I can convince her that I'm getting better is for the notch to go up on the scale? It's like the ends don't add up. It's not as black and white as I wish it could be. More weight should equal more happiness, but it doesn't—so why add pounds to unhappiness?

I'm keeping all these thoughts inside me, of course. If I ever want to escape Becca with my sanity intact, I've got to play it calm and collected. It's all about the show you put on. Diane always told me I should be in the plays at school.

MORGAN MENZIE

7.30.97

I am so sick of getting better. Becca said this would happen and I despise her for that. I don't have to live by her rules or anybody else's. I'm sick of fighting a battle I'm not going to win, and I'm sick of being sick!

It was much easier not fighting it. I want to just surprise them all. I want to do something unpredictable, something rash—just to get a rise out of everyone. I'm sick of people talking to me in a half-whisper, and I'm sick of having my parents watch my every move. I quit!

It doesn't help that Diane has apparently grown into a totally different person this year. She's grown braver and now I have no one left to fool! I know that I've said that I want this for her, but my goodness, can't I catch a little break? She still hugs me and prays for me, but there's this new side to her that I can't pin down. It's like she's perfectly content. That's what it is—contentment!

She's a lot stronger than I could have ever imagined. She doesn't wish to be anything but herself, and this makes her eerily calm and it drives me crazy! But what's worse is that I'm so darn happy for her. I want to be mad and jealous that she's reached this new place in her life, but I just can't help being glad. We must really be best friends if I love her when she vexes me most. More than anything I want to be happy for her, but this feeling of jealousy keeps creeping up on me. I smile, but it feels fake. I try to push it down, but this resentment keeps rising because she gets to feel good and have her little transformation into a better person without suffering like I have been.

I can't even be as good a friend as she is.

7.31.97

That's it! I'm packing my bags and moving to Scotland. It's about time I made that trip anyway—now that Diane doesn't need me, and I certainly have no boy holding me back. Becca and I can still converse via e-mail, and I can go somewhere that offers my own version of recovery: solitude.

I suppose being from the country, or the city for that matter, would give your life color—you know that thing they always use in literature classes to analyze novels. It's the point at which the author gets slammed. You raise your hand to say that you rather like the New England setting of *The Cider House Rules* only to be bull-dozed by the question of "Yes, but does it have color?" There's no true answer to that question, which I rather like, but which those teachers stubbornly refuse to acknowledge. All I know is, I would rather be anyplace in any one of those novels than here in mindless suburbia, growing up, then growing old in obscurity. They say that the Christians are a persecuted people and must constantly defend their faith. I say, "Where have you been, because here in the Bible Belt, tucked away in my private Christian academy, I am 100 percent average with zero chance of ever catching anything as exciting as a theological debate. Mom says I take life too seriously. She says I'm only fourteen years old and that I shouldn't worry about such matters. I say I've already had fourteen years to warm up and I am ready to go.

Anyway when I suggested this to Becca, she just eyed me and said, "Do you think your problems won't follow you there?" Oh, she infuriates me! I feel like a trapped animal. Why doesn't God help me?

God, why don't You help me?!

8.7.97

Life hangs suspended in the air,
Smoldering and whipping in the wind.
Ashes fall like snowflakes,
To cover the ground with the purity of shame.
Plains of gray leave us breathless,
For to inhale would be to relive . . .
No one wants that . . .
So life smolders on.

I guess I'm just tired of having to swim through the past in order to figure out my future. Why does it have to be such a slow process? I feel like every step I take leads me to another fork in the road. Oh no, I can't just ignore that little path off to the side, I have to assess it, note the changes in wind, and every minute decide if I want to get better or worse.

My life is not as clear-cut as it used to be. It consisted of black and white, of schoolwork and food. Now my life is full of gray. Emotions bring too much murkiness to the water. I feel more lost and confused than ever.

When am I going to figure this thing out?

8.9.97

Weight: 110
Calorie intake: 500

My weight is finally up. Great. Now what am I?

It's all a healing process. Everything that happens in life is just another step in the infinite twelve-step plan. I know all about recovery—how to speed it up, slow it down, fake it, live it, really feel it until it shakes you to your core, and all that used to be solid for you now floats, suspended in the air like fruit in Jell-O.

Everybody's healing from something. Usually something they brought upon themselves—I am one of those. I am sick of healing. I need some more action. I'd rather be confined to a hospital room with one of those little blue plastic bracelets on my fragile wrist that reads: "Beaumont, Marie Blythe" and states my condition, which I can't even name anymore because I don't feel thin or depressed enough to be anorexic. Yet I feel these deep tidal waves of self-doubt and self-consciousness.

I just hate myself because I'm what I always dreaded—average. I'm not cute, and now I'm not starving myself, so I've lost that desperate waif look to be replaced with what . . . melancholy average. I can't even create a unique name for myself. My whole being rages against falling back into my old way of life, and yet it'd be nice to take a little break.

I need an intermission. Life, however, is not a play or movie. I can't have music and leading men accompany me wherever I go. I need a miracle. I need God to either send me an adventure or calm me with His hand. I need Him to prove Himself to me. I need to be satisfied . . . with everything, including myself.

Maybe I need to write a book, anything to get my focus off of myself—oh, that'll be easy!

8.11.97

A Poem in Prayer

Lord, send me a Michael,
A Gabriel, an angel.
Lord, I need an adventure,
A novel, a love.
I need a peace, a joy, that glows.
Lord send me an angel
To let me know
That I'm on the right track,
That I'm heading the right way.
That I've finally got the knack
For making this life worth living.
Lord I need Michael's wings to surround me.
I need Gabriel to carry me through.
Lord I need a miracle
If you want me to be a
Testimony for you.
I need a story to tell
With a happy ending . . .
At least some ending.
I need inspiration, the beauty of life.
I need that wind beneath me,
So I can take flight
And fly with your angels
Into the safety of you.
I just need one hug,
One warm enveloping hug,
Softened by the tips of downy wings.
Just one hug to soar.
Amen.

I don't know if He'll hear me, but I know that I needed to say this. Whether I fight this thing for the rest of my life, or I am healed tomorrow, I needed to say this. I hope He hears me. He needs to know that I need help and that I'm about to chuck this whole Christian upbringing out the window if when I need Him most He deserts me.

8.30.97

Okay, I know I didn't do my food chart, but this is way more important than that and boy do I have an idea! Neither of them knows it yet, but I'm going to set Oliver up with Diane. Sometimes my foresight amazes me!

They're perfect for each other. I've been the middleman for so long that they don't really even know how perfect they are, but I can see it. Oliver has blond hair, which is a bit lighter than Diane's, and he has blue eyes that are a little lighter than mine. He runs cross-country, and Diane's a runner, too. The only thing stopping them from making the perfect couple is her shyness and his blindness of the situation.

Diane once asked me why Oliver and I never dated. We're just too close as friends and neither of us feels that way about the other. He's like a brother. But he and Diane, they are so right for each other and I have so much energy to spare lately that this will be the perfect project.

I think I'll break the idea to Diane first and then slowly accustom Oliver to it. He lives just down the road from me, so all I have to do is arrange for Diane to be at my house one night and drop the invitation to him as well and the rest will be history. Of course, I'll have to pick out an outfit for Diane. She never wears anything daring unless I force it on her. And I'll have to do her makeup, seeing as how she doesn't wear any.

Oh, I hope they'll let me give the toast at their wedding. I can tell all our closest friends and relatives how the two lovebirds fell in love under my spell . . .

9.15.97

Well, sad to say, I have no updates on the Diane-Oliver date scene. This is going to be harder than I thought. While eating lunch on the steps I casually said, "Don't you think Oliver has grown an awful lot over the summer? Both of you tower over me now."

"Oh, you're not that much shorter than I am. And I'm sure you'll keep growing long after I've stopped."

"Yeah, but don't you think Oliver has grown this past summer? He's really filled out. He looks like he could be a junior. You know I saw him looking at you in Latin the other day."

That was all it took to freak her out.

"What! Blythe, he was probably looking at you. Why would he be looking at me anyway?"

I just shook my head and changed the subject. Diane needs to get it into her head that she is an attractive girl, and Oliver is just the guy to make this happen. All good things come in time. That's another one of Grandma's sayings. I wonder if she ever fixed up her friends? Did they even know what "fixing up" was back then?

MORGAN MENZIE

9.25.97

Breakfast:
Who cares!

Lunch:
I don't know, why don't you tell me?

Dinner:
Whatever I please!

This is a big day for me, and I think we should all observe a moment of silence as the book of food logs closes for the last time . . .

Thank you! I have finally graduated from Food Chart Academy, and although I am still seeing Becca, it's only a matter of time until that, too, is crossed off the list. My weight has reached a desirable number and my food logs have been impressive if not pristine, although not entirely truthful. It doesn't matter now, for the lies stop with the food logs. I am happier than I have ever been. God must be in a really good mood. I found this verse in my Bible the other day:

When I kept things to myself,
I felt weak deep inside me.
I moaned all day long.
Day and night you punished me.
My strength was gone as in the summer heat.
Then I confessed my sins to you
and didn't hide my guilt.

I said, "I will confess my sins to the LORD."
And you forgave my guilt.

PSALM 32:3-5

Don't you see? All I had to do was ask Him to forgive me and heal me, and He did. That's all I had to do. Maybe Diane isn't the only one with access to God. Why else would I be happy and in the process of escaping Becca? He wants me out of there as much as I do. He knows that I am not truly sick. Even if I was sick, it wasn't for very long and it didn't grip me very deeply. God saw to it that I wasn't scarred by the experience, and He is now showing everyone because I am His child, and He was waiting for me to recognize it.

How can anyone look at me and not say that I am better?

10.13.97

Too much of me wants to close my eyelids and sink into a world of fairy tales. High school isn't all it's cracked up to be.

I am sick, literally gagged at the thought of another day at the academy, another A.P. test, another list of criteria in which I have to fit and yet somehow transcend in order to make a worthy scholar/human/contribution to society.

I say "too much" when really ALL of me wishes to be a part of that adventurous, hobbit-roaming, dragon-slaying, lush world. I want princes and talking horses and perpetual excitement of the utmost literary sense which always ends in something dramatic—as opposed to the life I am leading now which consists of a runny nose, avoiding the parents, a moderate high school tennis career, and a best friend who doesn't need me anymore.

Do I feel sorry for myself? Yes. Do I dream of a make-believe world in which my life is scrawled on yellowed pages? Yes! Do I realize that's never going to happen? Absolutely. Am I still going to wish and daydream every day? Absolutely. If I can't live in a make-believe world, can't I at least pretend or write my own? UNQUESTIONABLY!

May my A.P. Latin mid-term fall down the rabbit hole and drown in a sea of tears.

11.2.97

Hallelujah, praise the Lord! I am officially released from Becca's care. I'm back up to 120 pounds, and she says that I'm in full recovery. I had to hold back the tickle in my throat that wanted to say, "I was probably never really sick in the first place." This is how the conversation panned out:

"See this chart, Blythe? This downward slope is your descent into anorexia. You've come back out of that and now you're on this plane right here."

"Cool."

I saw that I was not at the end of the chart, but I hoped that if I didn't bring it up Becca wouldn't either. No such luck. She began telling me what the rest of the chart meant, but I zoned out and turned inward, thinking about somewhere far away. I didn't tune back in until she was finishing, "But what you need to remember is that falling back in doesn't put you back at the beginning; it's just part of your full way back to a healthy lifestyle. Don't be afraid to call me if you're having trouble. There's no shame in that."

"Oh, okay."

That's what I said, but this is what I was thinking: *You gotta be kidding. Now that I'm out there's no way I'm slipping back into nutritional counseling. Once I finish something it's finished for good. You're the one I need to recover from. And if you think I'm gonna call you to chat it up, you're out of your mind.*

I stood up and shook her hand. She tried to give me a hug, but I'm not a touchy-feely kind of person. I stepped out of that office, took one last look at the Batman chair, and walked as fast as I could just short of a run into the fresh air (or as fresh as can be expected downtown). I shook the stale-cigarette smell off my clothes and never looked back. I vow never to be back there again. And I'm a woman of my word.

MORGAN MENZIE

So congratulate me. I'm a new woman, and now I can move on with my life in a manner more to my liking. I don't need this baby-sitting any longer. There is a reason you fight for independence—to make a place for yourself in this world. My place is as far from Becca's office and Mom's worried looks as I can get. It's time to make a change. We'll see how they like the new me. I think I'll be a scholar for now, one who would do justice to my Scottish fantasy. I'll be more wise and mature than any of the ill-fated mentors in my life. It's time I claimed my place in this world. Carpe diem!

11.15.97

Okay, I know I am supposed to be working on Diane and Oliver, but Owen has surfaced again. I thought I was over him, especially after what happened with him and Liz. The warmth of his Valentine's gesture had faded into a temperate act by a temperate boy. But he lured me back in . . . this time with his cat.

I needed to escape from my parents, so I went to Grandma's house and spent the night and listened to old stories about how she and Pa met. She loves to tell how Pa (his name is William) rode up to her one sunny day on his black horse. She was fifteen, and when she looked up at that man in all black with his red hair glinting from under his cowboy hat, she knew he was the one. Pa just laughs and tries to get her to dance with him. Whenever he's in a good mood his feet start tapping, and there's no stopping him. He has his own version of dancing. It's somewhere between tap and square dance. Grandma usually just says, "Oh, sit down, you old man," but he spins me around the room instead. Somehow, my problems never seem important when I'm at their house, listening to the two of them tell stories and helping Grandma snap beans for dinner.

As you've probably guessed, my visits grew scarce when I decided eating was a bad idea. It was just too hard to lie to my grandparents about why I wasn't hungry or why I didn't want to get up to my elbows in flour and fish on fried catfish night. But since I've gotten well, my visits have increased and it's just like it used to be.

Anyway, one Saturday Grandma was teaching me how to make her famous coconut cake with homemade icing when I heard this meowing at the door. Well, actually I heard the dogs go crazy with barking before I heard the cat, but that's beside the point. Pa rounded the dogs up, and I went to see what was scratching at the front door.

MORGAN MENZIE

It was the cutest black and white cat I have ever seen. (It's only Dad's stubborn streak that has kept me from forming my own pet reserve.) I couldn't just shut the door on this cute creature, so I picked her up and instantly she began to purr like I was her long lost piece of tuna. I checked her tag and saw that she belonged to Owen. *Just my luck*, I thought.

After a few minutes of mental debate, I decided that it would be healing for me to return the cat personally. I felt I needed closure. I also wanted to show Owen that I was long over him. When he opened the door, I knew I was in trouble. I had spent so much energy trying not to notice him that I had forgotten how attractive he was. I felt the ice melting and in a desperate attempt to keep the fire of anger stoked I blurted out, "It's people like you who should never own pets! You just mistreat them and leave them to starve on the street!"

He stared at me blankly for a minute and then began to laugh, which made me equally embarrassed and furious. I didn't know whether to run the other way or yell at him.

In a restrained voice I asked him, "What's so funny?"

He just kept laughing. Finally he breathlessly said, "You've stuck yourself to Oreo."

It only took me a second to realize what I'd done. In the process of baking, I had gotten icing the consistency of melted marshmallow all over the front of me, and now that it was dried, the cat was stuck to me.

I was *so* embarrassed. I was a sophomore, standing on the doorstep of a boy's house, whose cuteness was undeniable, and I had a cat stuck to my shirt. The cat didn't even look flustered; she just went for the icing in ecstasy.

Owen helped me peel her off, and when it was all over we were both laughing, and I looked like I was wearing a black fur T-shirt. Oreo, on the other hand, didn't think it was so funny. Not only was she separated from the tasty icing, but her coat was quite thinned out on one side when it was all finished.

Tentatively, I asked him, "How's Liz?"

"I'm not really the person to ask since we're not dating anymore."

"Oh really," I responded innocently, "Why not? I thought you two made a perfect couple."

"Yeah well, I found out she has this strange aversion to hot chocolate, and I knew we could never get past it."

He grinned that lazy, arrogant grin, and I was embarrassed and angry all over again but for quite a different reason—he had reeled me back in. I was hopeless. It had been over a year since my infatuation had started, and all he had to do was smile and I was back to square one. The butterflies whirled in my stomach. We both smiled. And we have been together almost every day since then.

Grandma's beginning to get suspicious of all the time I'm spending at her house. She knows it's not just for the stories anymore. As far as Pa goes, he loves Owen. If he can get him cornered, he'll talk his ear off about lawn mowers and fishing. I've already decided he'd fit into the family nicely. Of course, he doesn't know any of this yet. All in good time.

What makes matters even more perfect is that he and Oliver have grown oddly close these past few months, and since I am Oliver's best friend it's only fair that he give me the inside scoop and drop hints for Owen along the way. Oliver doesn't know this yet, but it's only a matter of time before I break my plan to him.

Oh, the world is so much more exciting when you're in love.

MORGAN MENZIE

11.27.97

Thanksgiving Break

I've talked Mom and Dad into having Thanksgiving at Grandma's this year. This will give me the perfect view of Owen's house in case he wants to maybe go for a walk or watch football with me later. I better look cute.

Maybe I should drop a couple of pounds. Can I do that in a week?

I know those few pounds are the only thing keeping me and Owen apart. Of course, I can't ever tell anyone in my family this or they'll freak out and make me see Becca again, and I swore I would never go back there. So this is between me and the sacred pages of the journal. And I trust you to keep it hush-hush.

It's not like I'm going to go overboard or anything. Everybody talks about losing five pounds, especially around the holidays, so in reality I'm even *more* normal for wanting to make it happen. I think I might have just crossed another peak in the chart to my recovery.

This time I'm going to go about things much more responsibly. I'm going to pray all the way through it, and I know God will keep me in control so nothing bad will happen. I've mentioned this to Diane, and I can tell she doesn't think it's a good idea, but she would never say that. She's too afraid of making me mad.

Her new-found confidence has yet to affect me, and I can only pray that this will hold out.

12.2.97

I've begun to write letters to my future husband. I'm trying to write them without picturing someone in my mind, but I can't help but think of Owen. Here's the first one:

My Love,

I don't know what I'll do without you. You whom I've never met and will always love. You're out there living your life, and I'm here living mine. I see you in every picture. I hear you in every song. You make me smile with sadness knowing that you're gone.

You're out of reach and out of love, with me at any rate. Maybe you have a love and maybe she's grand, but don't you know that I'm the love of your life? Our hearts fit together. God made us to be one. Sometimes I try to picture how you'll look at me and smile and how you'll smell with your arms wrapped around me.

Sometimes you walk across my thoughts and dreams, glance at me and grin. You make me laugh as I want to cry, for I need you here with me. I ache inside at the thought of you, and I pray that God is watching your steps and watching mine and slowly guiding us together in his own time. I pray and I wait . . . and when my faith is wavering I search for that look in your eyes and that smile, but you're only in my mind for now.

But know that I love you, and I'm waiting for you to walk out of my dreams as God leads us to one another in this life and forever.

Love,
Blythe

P.S. Wait for me; I'm coming. Hold on tight to your heart and I'll hold on to mine, and we'll release them together and watch as they entwine.

Hmmm, this is probably better suited for a country song. Okay enough, all my heartfelt thoughts are turning into cheesy mush.

12.5.97

The Crazy Day That I'll Never Begin to Understand

It was so great at first. All my plans were coming together at the perfect climax. Diane and I were going to meet up with Oliver and Owen to go to the basketball game Friday night. All the people I love were going to be in the same place at the same time, so I could see all the plans unfolding before my eyes.

Diane had come over early so we could get ready together. She didn't see that there was any sense in getting ready at all. These were her words exactly when she showed up at my door, "It's only a basketball game. Why do we need to get ready two hours early? What are you up to?" Can you believe that? She was actually going to the game to meet the men we are going to marry and have children with in just an old seventies shirt of her mom's and, of course, no makeup. I clearly have my job cut out for me.

Now I don't want you to get the impression that I am this flashy girl who wears bright blue eye shadow and fluffs her hair. I would choose a T-shirt and jeans any day over dressing up, but this is such an important occasion that it ought to be special.

I put Diane in some clothes of mine. Nothing extravagant, just a soft green shirt that matched her eyes, and I let her wear her jeans. I pulled on a maroon sweater and camel corduroy pants, and put a little makeup on both of us. We were exactly on time for the game. The guys, of course, showed up late wearing T-shirts and shorts in the middle of winter. But I guess that means we're supposed to think they're tough.

The game was great. I mean I don't know what the score was or anything, but hanging out with the guys was great. Unfortunately, I ended up sandwiched between Oliver and

Diane. Owen was on the end, and I could sense that he was disappointed we weren't next to each other. He kept looking over Oliver and winking at me.

After the game we went to Dairy Queen. I was a little freaked out, but I knew I had to stick to my plan if Owen and I were ever going to end up together—that means no calories. So, I ordered a Diet Coke. Diane had a Blizzard, and the guys had sundaes. I think Owen admires my self-control.

When Mom came to pick Diane and me up, I caught Owen whispering something to Oliver. It was driving me crazy all the way back to the house. I had to know what he said. Diane said she thinks he likes me. She said she could just tell. But Diane always wants what's best for me, so she'll imagine whatever I need to hear.

We called Oliver to inquire about the whisper, and can you believe it? He wouldn't reveal anything. I told him:

"We have been friends for practically forever and you can't manage to utter a few words to appease me!"

"I don't think it's something he wants me to tell you."

"Oh, well aren't you the loyal friend. Too bad you desert the one and only person in the world who would tell you anything if you wanted to know."

"That's not fair. I can't tell, and you can't use guilt to make me. Why do you want to know anyway?"

"Because I just do."

"Oh, I'm supposed to tell you what he said, but you can't tell me why you want to know?"

"Fine. I like him, all right? I don't know how it happened, but I really, really like him. After that football game last fall, I had sworn to myself I wouldn't and I thought I could stick to it, but he's changed and he's much nicer. He just has the sweetest face and really deep brown eyes and . . ."

"Enough! I don't want to know! You know I'm your friend, but

I'm also a guy. And Owen is my best friend, so I don't want to hear about his brown eyes!"

"Fine, see if I tell you anything ever again! I thought you would help me, but instead you just get all weird. I don't want to talk to you anymore!"

"Fine!"

"Fine!"

Can you believe this was the conversation that ended what was supposed to be a glorious night? Diane agrees with me that Oliver is a traitor and the worst friend in existence. At least I know I'll always have her on my side.

12.26.97

Oliver and I haven't talked since that basketball game before Christmas break. I miss him. He frustrates me to death! Why does he have to be so stubborn? At first I tried to be nice and pretend nothing happened, but he wouldn't even look at me! It also doesn't help that Owen is distant lately. I tried to talk to him about Oliver, but it's like he's not even listening. Diane is the only one who I can stand right now, and I haven't even seen her in a week because she's been so busy with her family in town.

I've spent more time with my relatives in the past week and a half than all of my life up to it. We all went to Cracker Barrel yesterday and ate good ol' fried everything. I've been so down since the Oliver episode, I didn't even care what I ate. I just ate.

Pa and I played checkers by the fire while our food was being fixed. I beat him three out of five, but I think he let me win. I guess I've missed this time with all of them.

The cousins are bigger now and are much easier to take care of and the boys are finally beginning to realize I'm a girl and therefore have let up on the roughhousing. I kind of like the cloud of perfume, brightly colored sweaters, and shaving cream that hovers protectively around me. Each one has congratulated me on how good I look now. Grandma started crying when she saw me and said, "Why darling, you're as cute as a speckled pup under a red wagon." I'd never been so glad to hear those words.

Through all the happiness, a fear kept winding through me. I was happy that they were happy, but when left alone a sick feeling crept into my stomach. I am afraid to look "good." It's like when I'm around them, it's enough to see them happy. But when I am alone facing myself in the mirror it just isn't enough. I need to be thinner. I need it to make me satisfied—to ease my anxiety.

1998

1.1.98

It was just Diane and I this year. Oliver still isn't talking to me. We cut confetti like always and watched movies, although I don't remember what they were. I wasn't really paying attention to the plot. I was scrutinizing the actresses. And out of this study I have made a new Plan:

1. Don't worry about making others happy. Find happiness for me.
2. Happiness = losing weight. Therefore, don't eat until reach actress weight range.
3. Fortify my relationship with Diane and try not to care about Oliver.
4. Find out what Owen said!
5. visit grandparents and buy Pa a checkerboard.
6. Don't rant and go on and on and . . .
7. Smile more often.
8. Continue to succeed in school.
9. Stop chewing gum. Five calories a stick—it's not worth it!

1.5.98

In honor of this dreary month, I've been reading Hemingway. For some reason I can't get him out of my head. I am utterly fascinated. *A Farewell to Arms* is my new theme novel. It suits me perfectly. Fall in love with some dark hero and risk war, pestilence, and lunacy to run away with him and then die.

I'm Catherine. I am the tragic heroine. I give everything to a relationship and what do I get out of it? Nothing. I'm a terrific sufferer. Maybe that's my destiny: suffer in order to release beautiful and wise things into the world.

Speaking of suffering, it's been much harder this time around to work out the food plan. Normally I would just set a goal amount of calories I cannot exceed in a day and stick to it, but Mom has grown suspicious of me since the days of my so-called "disease," and it's harder to get around her.

She is determined to fix a family meal every night, but I know it won't last. The first time Dad says he can't eat until ten because he has a board meeting, or Mom's out with Grandma and loses track of the time, family dinners are off for good. I guess I'll just have to wait it out. I'm not a patient person unless it involves something very important to me. Right now I am the queen of patience.

And if God thinks He can just keep me here at this ridiculous weight of 120 pounds then I can out-wait Him, too. I can tell He's working against me, but when I set my mind to something it *will* happen. If these pounds are what's keeping me from happiness with Owen, then off they go.

Note to self: Toughen up. Your will has gotten soft in these months of self-indulgence. It's time to tighten the belt.

1.10.98

Look at what God threw in my face this morning!

> People can make all kinds of plans, but only the LORD's plan will happen.
>
> PROVERBS 19:21

And if that isn't bad enough:

> No one can control the wind or stop his own death. No soldier is released in times of war, and evil does not set free those who do evil. . . . No one knows what will happen next. Like a fish caught in a net, or a bird caught in a trap, people are trapped by evil when it suddenly falls on them.
>
> ECCLESIASTES 8:8; 9:12

He's trying to wear me down, but it's not going to work. And if He thinks I don't get the war allusion to Hemingway's novel, He's very much mistaken. If He wants to play this game, then I just won't read His stupid book any longer. I know He thinks He's the reason I haven't lost any of this weight, but I've got news for Him: new plan.

I leave for a fun-filled intense college-prep session at the prestigious Collins-Weatherby Academy in the spring. I will be spending a semester, three whole months, unsupervised. That's right: No more family meals, no more restriction of exercise, and no one watching over my shoulder. It's all downhill from there. So let God fight me all He wants; once spring term comes, I'm a free woman.

1.15.98

Well, I've finally got Oliver talking to me again. I've conceded that just because I like Owen doesn't mean I have to gush about him. On the pact that I swore *not* to gush over Owen, Oliver promised to help me with some insider information. He said he would work on him for me, and see how he feels about me. He still refuses to reveal the secret, but I am patient.

Because I'm back in the matchmaking business, I'm giving the Diane-Oliver idea a fresh start. This time, I'm going to tell Diane straight up that she needs to date him, because what could be more perfect than my two best friends dating each other?

I've started writing the toast I will give at their wedding.

1.19.98

I think I'll also break the God subject to Diane and see how she feels about Him. I mean, I know she's going to go on and on about the new stuff she's learned and how He's working in her life, but maybe if I listen real carefully I can figure out how she got Him to do all this stuff. It's not a question of whether I believe in Him or not, because I've decided I do. I suppose I have all along, but I guess I just want to know *why* i believe in Him. Why do I feel so guilty all the time? And why can't I just live in a hole in the ground in the middle of the desert?

Anything would be better than being surrounded by these superficial people who occupy my school. They walk through the halls telling nobody in particular a bit too loudly how God has worked in their lives lately. They raise their hands at church camp and pray the longest before lunch, but none of them have ever undergone anything to make them question their faith or make it real.

It's like saying you're a diehard Democrat just because your parents are when you can't even vote and you know nothing about the candidates. I just can't stand them, because I know they are phonies—and there's nothing in the world I hate more than phony people.

Especially when it comes to God.

I mean, He knows whether or not you're lying. Fooling regular people isn't going to get you anywhere, and you can't fool God—so what's the point? I may not particularly like Him right now, but at least I let Him know it instead of pretending He and I are just peachy when I don't know the first thing about Him. Diane isn't phony; she doesn't flaunt her faith. She is absolutely perfect in comparison to me.

But anyway, I wrote a speech that I would read to all these hypocrites if I could. I would stand up in front of a huge podium and point my finger at each and every one of the "suffering souls" who walk down the hall . . . Enough ranting; I swore to myself that I would never ramble or rant. It's in The Plan, and I'm going to stick to it.

1.25.98

It's only a few days until I leave for the Academy and can really focus on fulfilling The Plan. I hope this will be an opportunity to cross things off the list one by one. I haven't told Diane The Plan (shedding the weight that is keeping Owen and me apart), and I don't intend to. She doesn't need to know something that will only hurt her and cause her to worry. And I know her; she will worry. We're alike in that way: born worriers. And the fact that she'll silently worry and not say anything to me or anyone else will not be good for her. Knowing that she is upset will only make me upset.

Anyway, I'm not any good at lying to her; I'm so used to telling her everything. So I've formed a way around lying: silence. I must be completely silent on any food issues. I must not utter a single syllable about food in these next few days, and if she happens to bring it up I will remain close-mouthed. It might seem odd to her that I suddenly become mute, and in that case she will nervously change the subject, swiftly bypassing the lie. She's used to me doing odd things like that anyway, so my silence won't seem *that* unusual.

Now that Diane is taken care of, the parents are going to be a little bit more difficult. I can handle Mom. I can always handle Mom. But Dad is a different story. He's more aggressive, more direct. He can tell when I'm lying. He's going to want to discuss the trip and all the issues it might bring up. He's going to order me not to get sick again, and he's going to watch me like a hawk until I leave.

It's a good thing he's so excited about the trip: you know, "his daughter being smart enough to get into the elite pre-college session that looks so good on the transcript." If I'm lucky, he'll be too distracted by my smarts to notice a change in my behavior, and I'll quietly blend into the background when he is around until it is time for me to leave.

I must avoid conflict at all cost!

1.27.98

I'm a little disappointed in Owen. For someone who I had pegged as madly in love with me, he is not very concerned about my departure. I've tried to call him since we got out of school, and he's been too busy to talk for more than five seconds every single time. I ended up leaving him my address at school and hanging up in the middle of his excuse of why he can't chat this time.

The ball's in his court now.

If he writes me, he's back in my good graces and if not, I'm moving on to someone better. If he was never really interested in the first place, well then fine with me, I'll just have to find romance while I'm away.

Speaking of romance, I talked to Diane about Oliver and she completely freaked out, but I'll just give her some time to get used to it and everything will sort itself out. I'm warming him up to the idea as well. I've gotten the three of us together a few times, but when I finally come up with an excuse to get away, they both cling to me like lost kittens at the prospect of being left alone with each other. That, of course, is all going to change when I leave for a month. They will just have to do stuff together, at my plea. I've already drafted a sample beginning to each of their letters:

Dear Diane,

I am afraid Oliver is getting lonely without me there to keep his life exciting. Because I know you're a good friend, no, a best friend, I'm sure you will take good care of him while I'm away . . . "

Dear Oliver,

I've been talking to Diane and she sounds pretty lonely. She won't admit it, but because we're so close I can tell she misses hanging out with you. Maybe you two could get together and just talk. If it gets awkward, just call me and it will be like we're all three there, like always . . ."

That's all I've got so far, but I think it will work. I hope it will work.

Well, now all I have to do is move the right pieces and before you know it, it'll be checkmate.

1.31.98

One Day to Go

The Dance

1 2 3
don't stop now.
1 2 3
try a little harder.
1 2 3
you can do better than that.
1 2 3
hit the books.
1 2 3
never quit.
1 2 3
this is it.
1 2 3
the dance of your life.
1 2 3
don't screw it up.
1 2 3
do it for me.
1 2 3
keep on going.
1 2 3
never quit.
1 2 3
not perfect yet.
1 2 3
keep dancing, keep dancing.

1 2 3
never perfect, never right.
1 2 3
the dance of your life.
1 2 3
don't screw it up.
1 2 3
here's your finale.
1 2 3
finish with a bang.
1 2 3
the dance of your life.
1 2 3, 1 2 3, 1 2 3 . . .

Sometimes I wish I could just quit dancing. Quit school, quit pretending, quit fighting, quit losing, quit sinking deeper. I'm tired, and I'm ready to stop.

God, why can't it be time to stop?

2.1.98

Collins-Weatherby

I cried almost the whole way up here. I couldn't help it. All the times I've wished to be somewhere else, anywhere else, it seemed a faraway impossibility. Now that it is here I don't want to do it. I didn't want to leave Mom, and my confidence has withered to nothing. The car was packed with all my stuff, and Mom was driving me exactly where I'd wanted to go for months. But when we actually left home, and I knew I wouldn't be going back with her, I began to cry. I'm fifteen years old and I cried over leaving my mommy for four weeks!

I guess my confidence only exists on home turf. The whole way she kept trying to get my mind off of it by chatting the way she does when she gets sad or nervous, but I just kept crying. The closer we got, the further I scrunched into the seat, hoping my body would stick there and Mom would be forced to take me back home.

About twenty minutes from our destination, it started to rain. It was a sign from God that this is not where I am supposed to be. I told Mom that, but she just ignored me by saying that we'd find a real close parking spot and I'd feel better once I was settled in.

When we arrived Mom was true to her word. We got as close as possible to those dented metal doors leading into the dormitory corridors. Mom and I lugged all my stuff, wet and wrinkled, inside where a florescent gloom clung to the walls and illuminated every crevice of structure and man. We could have walked into an insane asylum! My room, 216, was pretty close to the door. Mom said it was luck. I said "perfect for the criminals to sneak in."

My roommate had already arrived and settled in on the other

MORGAN MENZIE

side of the room. She occupied the bed next to the window. I was left next to the door. She had cartoon posters on the walls and funky stuffed animals all over her bed. She wasn't there, and I was glad. While I was unpacking and still crying a little, Mom found the scale that I had stored in the very bottom of my bag. She wasn't meant to find it. I was planning to take it out after she had gone, but I had to play it off now. When she looked at me all worried and asked me why I needed this, I just told her that it was to monitor my weight so that I was sure I didn't lose any. She didn't say anything after that . . . except that she thought she remembered Becca saying that scales only escalated problems for people with food issues.

My anger at Mom for finding the scale still didn't overcome my sadness at the prospect of her leaving. We had a few hours before orientation, so I begged her to take me somewhere off campus. It was not until we left the pavement and mowed grounds that I realized I was in the middle of nowhere. The only civilization for miles around was a Wal-Mart Supercenter, and tiny movie theater with rocking chairs. In between these three complexes were a few scattered fast-food restaurants of no-name standards.

This was the thriving metropolis I was to live in for the next thirty-one days. I began to cry again as Mom pulled into the parking lot of one of these fast-food dives. While she ordered, I calmly pulled out my diet root beer and bagel and began to nibble. When she came back she asked me why I didn't want anything. I just said I wasn't in the mood.

After this we went to Wal-Mart and bought a rug to cover the stained tiles and dirty crevices of the dorm room floor. Then there was nothing more to do but go back to the place that I already dreaded.

2.2.98

When we entered the auditorium for orientation yesterday, I stared into a sea of unknown faces. Instinctively I shrank into Mom's side until we were seated, and even then I kept holding her hand. "This isn't like you," she kept saying. "You are always outgoing and friendly." Maybe the old me was, but this new me didn't like the look of these people. And besides, she seemed to be forgetting that I have attended the same school since kindergarten.

I heard little of the talk, for I was too consumed in my own misery. I was counting the minutes until Mom had to leave. As we stood outside the back door of the dorm, we both cried. Mom kept saying that it was going to be okay and that I should go inside and meet my roommate. I kept saying that I didn't care if I ever met my roommate because all I wanted to do was go home with her. It started to rain again as she pulled away. I was soaked by the time I watched the car disappear in the distance.

My roommate ended up being okay. She is a year older than I am, as are most of the kids here. They will all be seniors, and I will only be a junior. That's what I get for overachieving. She has bright red hair and is very, very pale, which she accentuates with whiteout-colored powder. Her name is Erin, and she's about as social as I am.

We had to dress up for dinner tonight because it was the formal welcome to all the promising *youngsters*, as the chancellor called us. The dinner included some sort of beef and noodles, which I didn't touch. When Erin and I got back to our room, I ate a bagel. She laughed and said, "Oh I'm glad you're eating something. Ha! I was afraid I'd been stuck with some anorexic." I just laughed back to her and threw away the rest of my bagel.

Somehow I had lost my appetite.

MORGAN MENZIE

2.3.98

Today was a little better than the first two. We started classes today, so now I have something to keep my mind off home. I've developed a schedule of sorts:

Morning:
Get up, go to the bathroom, weigh myself.
Apple for breakfast.

Noon:
Change into running clothes immediately after 11:00
class, then eat a quick bowl of cereal and head
off to run: three miles around the track, then
back for afternoon classes—no time to change.

Evening:
Shower after classes or lay out to get some sun
and then shower, do homework until dinner at
5:30 where I arrive precisely as the doors open,
eat cereal or a bagel and then back to the room
for more homework.

It's good to have a schedule. I feel more secure now. I still cry a lot and call Mom and Dad every day, if not twice a day. I haven't picked up my spirits enough to look for any cute guys, but I have written Owen a long letter, trying to sound cheerful and full of worldly wisdom.

I've written Diane, too, but I'm not pretending to be okay with her. I told her pretty much everything, including how miserable I am. I even cried on the letter while I was writing and made it smear, which I tried to fix, but I know she's going to notice it and worry about me. Maybe she'll start praying for me again. I wouldn't mind that so much.

But I do have some good news, which I think is going to be my saving grace during this imprisonment: I feel as though I've lost weight. I know it's only been a few days, but tomorrow I will weigh to prove myself right. I think this just might be the perfect way to lose it anyhow. I've lost my appetite since I've been so sad, and it's much hotter here than it is at home, so the running simply sweats off the pounds.

I hope Owen will notice when I get back. I've just got to keep it up. I've started a tally of days. The cheap little calendar they gave us upon arrival has become my sentence count. The best part of the day is right before I go to bed, when I take my red pen and cross off the day.

I can handle this if I just take it one day at a time and focus on the goals I've set for myself. I will survive this and come out looking better than ever before.

2.21.98

It's not the circumstances themselves that shape our character—it's how we interpret those circumstances.

—MARIE BLYTHE BEAUMONT

The Wink

Time slips, I slip.
Tomorrow's a new day . . .
It's just the same.
The dice are cast,
The pattern set,
Won't somebody throw me a net?
Life goes on, so do I.
I swim and swim,
Yet where's the top?
I've sunk too low,
my life's a mess,
Why am I sick in my perfectness?
No one knows through pretty eyes,
A smile, a shrug and then no more
They're all fooled,
And so am I,
I wink at myself with my own eye.

I'm tired and ready to quit the game I've set up for myself, but I can't. I can't because I'm not a quitter, and I don't know how to fail. I can't because by now there's too much riding on this. The stakes are too high, and I don't know how to stop it without everything crashing down around me.

3.6.98

Dreams . . . how many dreams are out there, swirling in the atmosphere, mingling with oxygen, stars, and earth? How many wishes on candles and falling stars have burned out with the light of their source?

People walk around on a mission—a sad mission—to forget the dreams that were nourished in youth. They feign happiness in the face of success, labor, and THE MONOTONY OF LIFE.

There are too many abandoned dreams. Why doesn't someone reach up and grab one, fashion a net out of optimism, youth, passion. Braid the threads of childhood, carelessness, and lazy Saturdays into a web of hope in which the dreams will naturally fly.

Happiness is not an impossibility; it just requires a little imagination.

3.7.98

Weight: 130
Calorie intake: 450
Exercise: none

I was lying in the grass last night out behind the dorm because I couldn't sleep. I haven't been able to sleep for a while now, but I don't care because I burn more calories when I'm awake. With my flashlight and journal I wrote what I was thinking and that last entry is what came out.

I think I might be going mad from lack of sleep. Colors are brighter, but lines are blurrier. When I run, I'll go from weighty hotness to a floating coolness. The legs that were at one moment heavy as logs seem to take flight, and I'm running on air. A breeze picks up and I float along until the heat takes back over, and I sink to the ground with a greater force than before.

That's usually when I trip, after the heat thrusts me to the ground. Insomnia is kind of cool in a way. I am a girl who would never take drugs, I just couldn't do that to my body, but sometimes I imagine that this is what it must feel like. Dreamy and surreal. I don't think I'll tell my parents that I haven't been sleeping when Parents Weekend rolls around. They don't need to worry, especially when it's the only enjoyment I get out of this "intellectual experience." Even the writing I have to do here doesn't cheer me up. I'd rather be writing in this journal at home than writing dry papers here. Critiques always cheapen the experience.

3.15.98

Weight: 118
Calories: 300
Exercise: ran 3 miles

How cool is that?! I had no idea I had lost this much weight! The batteries on my scale were dead and it wasn't until today, Saturday, that I could get to Wal-Mart for some more. Seven pounds in seven days! If I keep this up, I'll look great by summer. Erin and even some of my professors that I saw around campus noticed how happy I looked today. I think I was beaming.

I've also discovered a way to work in a treat every now and then, so I can keep up the good work. Every Sunday for lunch I'll walk to Baskin Robbins, which is located in the same area as Wal-Mart and the theater. I am allowed one scoop of low-fat Maui Brownie Madness, and that is my lunch and dinner.

I read somewhere that an occasional dose of sugar boosts your metabolism and allows you to burn more calories if only for a limited time. Besides, I don't think I could make it this whole month without a few treats now and then. Plus, if Dad asks how I've been eating I can say, "Great actually! I just had Baskin Robbins this past Sunday," and I won't be lying.

Sometimes I can talk Erin into coming with me, which gives me an even better story because it shows my parents that I'm being social and happy. And when they think I'm happy they leave me alone. Of course, Erin thinks that this is just dessert and that I've already had lunch, which actually works out to my benefit here. When it's time for dinner I can just say, "Oh I'm not that hungry; I had a huge lunch *and* ice cream."

3.20.98

Boy, it's more exhausting keeping up with all these pretences than it is losing the weight. I really do wish I could just run away to the middle of nowhere and write and be happy and, most importantly, be totally devoid of human contact. Maybe I'll buy a houseboat and live on the sea. Hemingway would appreciate that. I would catch fish to eat and lay out on the deck all day just writing. Someday I'll spot a ship, which has obviously been lost at sea, and I'll sail my home over to investigate. And there will be the man of my dreams, eternally grateful for my rescue and enraptured by my beauty.

He will be chivalrous like the medieval days, and he will fish for us and we will live on the boat and raise our children there where no one can bother us. The kids can string up Christmas lights for no particular reason other than ambiance. And I'll read the stories I have written for them by the red and orange and blue hues cast by the lights as they fall asleep on the deck in my arms.

We'll sail around the world in our own castle on the sea and be free of everything that is wrong with the world.

(And Diane will be there, too, in her own boat with her own family, and maybe we will be mermaids like we used to pretend in my swimming pool.)

3.28.98

Weight: 115
Calories: 300
Exercise: 3 miles of sprints

I hate boys! I got a letter from Oliver yesterday. I had decided to try one last time to get out of him the secret that Owen whispered that night in December. I made a promise to myself that if he didn't tell me this time I would give up the chase and get over it. It figures that I would finally get what I want, and it's not what I wanted at all.

He starts the letter by telling me what's going on at home and how classes are going. I have to admit I skipped this first part, intending to read it later. I scanned the letter for any word on Owen, since Owen himself hadn't written me.

When I saw his name I practically jumped and then grew anxious in anticipation of news of any kind. I did not expect to find out the secret:

> . . . Well, I have something to tell you about Owen. I know you remember that night after the basketball game when we all went out. And I know it's been driving you crazy that I couldn't tell you what he said. But you'll soon understand why I couldn't, or wouldn't. Since you've been gone, he's been hanging out with Liz a lot. It didn't seem to be that big of a deal to anyone, but they didn't know what I knew. Even after they kept going out a lot, I hoped it was nothing. But yesterday he kissed her.
>
> Blythe, when we were in the parking lot and your mom was picking you and Diane up, Owen told me to flirt with you and distract you so that he could find

MORGAN MENZIE

Liz. I guess that was his stupid way not to hurt you. Of course, I wasn't going to do it because we're just friends, but I also didn't want to tell you until I absolutely had to. And then last night happened with him and Liz and I had to.

I'm sorry,
Oliver

I couldn't believe it! Liz and Owen again! I could have handled anything but that. Oh—they deserve each other: one shallow person for another. Yeah right, he was trying to save my feelings. You want to save my feelings? Don't kiss Liz! And Oliver didn't even warn me. If it were Diane, she would have warned me immediately. Oh, I hate boys!

4.1.98
April Fool's Day!

Weight: 114
Calories: 300
Exercise: ran 3½ miles

Parents Weekend is this week, and Mom and Dad are coming up on Saturday. It's really not fair that they call it Parents *Weekend* when they only get to spend the day here. But I'm actually okay with it. It's going to be hard enough to hide the weight loss for a few hours. I think I'm going to wear my overalls, that ought to do the trick.

My goal is not to cry when I see Mom. I've just missed her so much, and life is hard without any of her comforts. I miss her hugs in the morning and how we used to sit out on the porch and swing. I haven't done those things in over a year now. When I'm home I just don't feel like dealing with anyone, even Mom. But it's all going to be different when I get back. I'm going to show both my parents how much I love them and appreciate them. I just hope they don't bother me about this food stuff. Dad's the one I must be extra careful around. I've got to be discreet, and I've got to keep a smile on my face or he'll suspect something.

The thing is, this Sunday is Dad's birthday, and I've written a letter for him. It's sort of a poem, but I'm dreadfully afraid to give it to him. Dad and I have never been really close. It is always Mom who I go to when I'm having troubles, and the troubles are usually with Dad. We are too much alike; we get on each other's nerves.

I can tell when he's getting mad because I'm the same way, and I know just how to make him mad. I just think of what it would take for me. I think we either play with each other's emotions or avoid them all together. He's either at the office in his president mode, playing golf with associates, or working out while I'm at school, at tennis practice, or holing myself up in my room to do work.

Sometimes I get the urge to just sit him down and have a talk, but then I get intimidated. So I go to Mom and tell her all my complaints. I wish we could just be honest and relaxed around each other, but I spend the whole time wondering what he's thinking and worrying about what to say next. It's almost like his life is too big and full to accommodate me. I'm just a distraction. Mom is easier to be with. She's Mom.

The thing is, I just love him so much, but I don't know how to show it. Maybe it's because he's not good at showing it either. From the day I was born, Mom's been all hugs and loving, but Dad's a little harder to reach. Somewhere along the way it grew more awkward for us to hug, and now it's awkward just to talk. I want us to be close, and I won't give up until we are. I hope my letter lets him know how I feel.

4.2.98

Weight: 113
Calories: 300
Exercise: ran 4 miles—extra restless energy

I've been looking for something to get my mind off this weekend, and I might just have found something: His name is Tim. He works on the Academy newspaper, which I joined to test and refine yet another aspect of my writing, and we've talked a few times. He's so cute. He has ash blond shaggy hair that curls a little at the ends, and his eyes are the bluest-blue I've ever seen. He's lean because he's a swimmer, and he's tall, or at least it feels like he is when we're talking, which is all that matters anyway.

We're working on a story together. A Holocaust survivor is coming to campus to tell her story, and it's our job to interview her. I think I'm more nervous about being around Tim than the woman.

He's originally from Utah, but his family moved down South a few years back. He has *seven* brothers and sisters! He sings for the choir at his church, and he has the most amazing voice. I think I could listen to him forever. Of course, he doesn't know I like him. He's such a big flirt with everybody, and I flirt back like all the rest. I guess I'm hoping my flirting sinks in.

It's been a while since I felt this way about anyone. I know I didn't feel this good around Owen. Tim just makes me feel happy to be me. We have fun together, and I laugh more than I've ever laughed in my life when I'm around him.

Of course, I immediately told Diane, and she's so excited for me. She says he probably likes me back. She's never laid eyes on him, yet she is convinced he's in love with me. What a great friend! I told Oliver, too, and I think he's happy for me. But just like my crush on Owen, he said he would prefer that I not talk to him about it.

I immediately got offended and hung up on him, which was probably not the best move. He's my best guy friend, and he's beginning to censor our conversations. No, I am definitely not ready to apologize to him. Because I'm mad at him, my efforts to unite him with Diane have waned a bit. I casually asked her if she and Oliver had been keeping each other company. She said, "Yes, but it's kind of weird. I love you, Blythe, and you're my best friend, but I think you're going to have to give up this whole me-and-Oliver thing."

This was very forceful for Diane so it took me a minute to digest what she had said. I'm actually kind of proud of her for standing up for herself to me, because I know I can be pushy. Well, mostly proud, with just a tinge of hurt. After all, isn't this what I've always wanted?

I am still happy for her though, and I'm going to give up on her and Oliver because she asked me to. Besides, I'm not exactly in the mood to bring him any happiness at the moment.

Okay, back to a fresher and more cheerful subject: Tim. We're meeting tonight in the lobby of the dorm to go over our notes and questions for the Holocaust survivor. I haven't decided what I'm going to wear, but I can tell you this: I'm glad I shed a few of those unwanted pounds.

Tim said he doesn't decide whether he likes a girl by her looks, but he always points out cute girls, so I know he's lying. Not exactly lying, because I don't think he realizes what he's doing. But nevertheless, I'm glad I'm a little smaller than I was.

4.4.98

Weight: 109
Calories: Who knows?!

Parents Weekend

This was probably the worst day since the day I was born. I was so excited to see Mom that I got up way too early. I pulled on my overalls and the loosest shirt I could find and went to sit on the brick wall in front of the dorm to wait.

Well, I waited for what felt like forever, and because everything makes me emotional nowadays, I began to cry. I tried to hold it in, but I just kept thinking that they forgot to come or something happened to them. I was blubbering all over the place in plain view of the world to see, and probably Tim, when somebody tapped on my shoulder.

It was Mom. They had parked out behind the side entrance to the dorm because my room was right there. While I was sitting out front feeling sorry for myself, they were in the car around back waiting for me to come meet them.

One look at Dad and I could tell he was in a bad mood; he's about as good at waiting as I am. But at that point I couldn't stop crying, once I get myself going it's Niagara Falls, and before I know it I'm over the edge without a paddle. That's another one of Grandma's sayings: over the edge without a paddle. Well anyway, Dad wanted to walk around the campus, and since I couldn't stop crying or explain why I was crying in the first place, Mom stayed back with me.

I just hugged her for the longest time, not saying anything. When I finally looked up, she had this sad, worried face. It was the same face I had seen when I took the scale out of my bag. That's when I knew I had to suck it up or they would catch on.

MORGAN MENZIE

I cheered up and took Mom on a tour of the campus. We caught up with Dad, and I convinced them to take me somewhere off campus. Dad had done his research on the town and was prepared. He knew of a pretty good hiking trail not far from here. I knew I could always count on Dad to incorporate exercise into any outing. I had planned ahead and skipped breakfast because I knew lunch would be under the watchful eye of my parents, and it had to look like I ate normally.

The hike was not exactly what any of us expected. First of all, it was an hour's drive to the site because, as I've already mentioned, I am in the middle of nowhere. The trail consisted of planks hammered together in a haphazard manner to cover a treacherous swamp area that emitted a not-so-pleasant odor. I tried to make jokes about it, but even Mom wasn't in the mood for small talk. That's when I knew things weren't perfect in Oz. They knew something, or suspected something, of my behavior, and it was only a matter of time before the subject was broached.

We continued our hike, none of us saying what we were really thinking. The dark woods and murky waters seemed to fit all our moods. Dad was far ahead as usual, and I was lagging behind with Mom. That's when I noticed a path leading off to the left. The wood looked older than the planks we were walking on, and it aroused my curiosity.

I dragged Mom with me along this rickety path until we came to an opening in the woods. It was still dark: nothing could penetrate this gloom. But I managed to make out what looked like crates stacked on top of each other in the middle of the swamp. Upon closer inspection, I realized these were cages, and they were holding some sad-looking creatures.

By this time, Dad had retracked and was close behind me. He made a depressed sound in the back of his throat, and I turned with a question in my eye. He said that these were wild fowl that belonged to these parts, and these cages must be set up for tourists to learn about the wildlife.

I turned back to these cages which looked neglected and worn. I looked through the bars to see birds that looked even worse. There must be someone who looks after them; the doors to their captivity had fresh locks on them. Something in me swelled up in my throat until I felt like I couldn't breathe.

I began to cry again, and Mom said we should leave. In some stupid act of desperation I tried to reach out for the bird closest to me. She lunged at my hand with a ferocity I did not imagine was possible in something so scrawny. Dad said we should leave them alone and get back to the car. I let them lead me away, looking at my feet the entire time.

We drove to a restaurant for lunch. I don't remember the name—there are so many others just like it. As we sat down to look at the menus Dad said, "You must be hungry, Blythe, after we walked so far. You better eat a good lunch."

I wanted to slide off the high-gloss booth and slink under the table. Instead I just smiled at him and said, "Actually I'm not that hungry. I had a big breakfast." I ordered a salad, which I knew had full-fat dressing on it. I could tell from the film it left in my mouth. I ate about half of it, and then said I was full and we better be getting back anyway.

Mom tried to hug me on the way out to the car, but I pushed her away. I don't know why. I desperately wanted to hug her, but I did it anyway and retreated to the back seat of the car without a word.

The whole ride back to campus I thought of the birds. Those poor birds left not to die, but to suffer. They looked so sad. I wish I never had to deal with people again.

By the time we got back to campus, it was raining outside and I was in my own world above the rain, above the clouds, where I soared with the birds. Mom hugged me good-bye, and it felt

MORGAN MENZIE

awkward. Dad didn't even try. He just patted me on the back. As I was about to exit the car, Dad and Mom grabbed my hands and told me to sit down. They wanted to talk to me. This is how it went:

"Your mother and I have noticed that you don't look good, Blythe. You look too thin, and I want to know what's going on."

"Nothing is going on, Dad. I've just been running a lot and the food here is gross. But I ate good today."

"No you didn't. You didn't even eat half of your salad, and there's absolutely no protein in that. We probably hiked twice that amount in calories. And it scares me to think that what you ate for lunch today was normal. That portion was not normal. The way you pick at your food is *not* normal."

"We just want you to be healthy and happy, and when I saw you today waiting for us on that wall I knew you weren't happy."

"I am happy; I'm fine. You're the ones who wanted me to go here, and now you . . . all you can do is say mean things when you come to visit!"

I was crying.

"Blythe, people who are happy don't cry all the time."

"Mom, you don't understand. Neither of you understand how hard this thing has been for me. You send me off to this college thing, and I know it's an honor to be chosen, but it's all this work, and I don't know anyone here!"

"Now, stop crying. That's not going to get us anywhere. We can't talk if you don't stop crying."

"Well maybe I don't want to talk!"

With that I jumped out of the car, ran into the building and didn't look back. Who are these people who have stolen my parents' bodies and aim to sabotage me? I don't know what I'm going to do now, but I do know that they can't make me eat. I've got to fight with everything in me. If they think they can make me do anything they are wrong.

Next time they see me I'll be twice as thin!

4.8.98

Weight: 105
Calories: couple hundred

I have a week and a half left until I go home. I'm going to have to up everything a notch. I've also amended The Plan to help me get through these next eleven days without losing my mind and without breaking my spirit. The goal is to lose as much weight as possible in 264 hours, *but* at the end of that time I have twenty-four hours to eat whatever I want before I'm back on The Plan. This gives me a treat for surviving this horrible place, and it allows my parents to see me eating normal the first day or so I'm home. It's just enough time to satisfy my parents so that they turn the eagle-eye away from me, and I can resume my business.

I don't know what this means for Tim and me. They've planned a dance the last night we're here, as if we're twelve and at summer camp. I really want to go with him, and I've seen him goofing around dancing and he's pretty good. Of course I could never let myself dance, I'm too self-conscious and I feel stupid. But we could go together and talk, and hopefully we'll exchange numbers.

I just want him to think I'm cute. I hardly get to see him except when we're working on the paper because I'm either running or doing work. Friday's our big interview with the Holocaust woman, so maybe we'll go celebrate after that. I deserve a little happiness in the midst of all this suffering.

4.10.98

Weight: 100
Calories: stopped counting; goal: eat as little as possible.
Live off of diet drinks and fat-free popcorn.

Today was the interview. It threw off my timing a little bit because I usually run when we were supposed to meet the woman for lunch. But it was no big deal, I just got up at 5:00 and ran.

I bet I looked a little more tired than usual, but other than that, I made sure to wear my cute burgundy sleeveless top, which is a little tighter than my other clothes, and my black pants. I looked professional for the interview, yet attractive for Tim. I straightened my flyaway hair and pulled it back with a black leather headband. I was very impressed with myself by the time it was all finished.

I met Tim and the woman in the cafeteria at noon, and then we all got our food and sat down to chat. I wasn't used to eating the food because I usually skipped lunch to run, so it took me a little longer to choose what I thought would be the least caloric.

They were patiently waiting when I finally sat down with a small bowl of salad. There was vinaigrette at the salad bar, so I discreetly poured some of my water over my lettuce so they would think I had dressing. I was a little worried because the dressing is thicker than water, but I just set my glass in front of my bowl so that neither Tim nor the woman had a direct view.

After we ate and cleared the table, the woman, Ester, began her story. Both Tim and I took notes, and it all went very smoothly . . . until it all fell apart.

Ester was describing her experience in the concentration camp in Germany. She told how they were forced to stand outside in the freezing cold for hours on end, and they lined up while the soldiers walked back and forth yelling insults.

She told of the fleas that inhabited her mattress, which she shared with four other prisoners. As she described the barracks, which hardly offered shelter from the cold, I thought of the birds in the middle of the swamp sitting in their cages, weak and humiliated at their plight. I was snapped back to attention when she pointed at me and said with her thick accent: "You, I was as thin as this one here. I was skin and bones by the time we were freed. I looked twenty years older than I was."

She meant no harm by it. She was absorbed in the memories from the past and I guess I offered the description that she was searching for, but I was mortified. I laughed politely and pretended to write something down so Tim couldn't see the tears in my eyes. When it was over, I excused myself as quickly as possible and ran out of the cafeteria. I ran past the buildings where I had sat for three weeks, and I ran past the dorm and the track. I ran until I came to a cornfield, which surrounded the campus, forming a sort of barrier to the outside world.

When I couldn't breathe anymore I sat in the middle of the crop in the deep-rutted earth. I cried until I couldn't cry anymore. How could she say something like that to me and not know that it would hurt me? How could she think I looked like an emaciated prisoner of war? Not when I was so close to beautiful.

I lay among the cornstalks, exhausted from crying and running. I was exhausted from fighting the world for the right to eat or not eat what I wanted. I was tired of pretending and lying. I was tired of not talking to my family and not letting them into my life.

I don't know how long I lay there, but when I opened my eyes again it was getting dark. I heard a rustling about five feet from where I lay. This was what God was going to do; he was going to send some horrible animal to put me out of my misery so I could go to heaven and leave this stupid world. When I had resigned my life to that of animal food, a face popped through the stalks. It was Tim.

MORGAN MENZIE

"Hey kid, how are you? I've been looking for you for hours."

"Oh I'm sorry, Tim, I forgot we were supposed to meet and go over our notes."

"Listen, don't worry about it. Are you okay?"

"No, well sort of, I don't know; I'm just confused right now."

"Is it because of what Ester said?"

"Yeah, I guess I just don't see myself as she saw me. I mean I didn't think I looked that bad."

"I didn't want to say anything because I know how sensitive you are, but I worry about you. I know we haven't known each other that long, but I guess I just don't want anything to happen to you."

This is where my pride kicked in.

"Nothing is going to happen to me; I can take care of myself."

With that I stood up abruptly—and fainted. It's a good thing Tim is quick, or I would have impaled myself on a cornstalk. He caught me and laid me on the ground. It took a few seconds for my vision to clear, and in those few seconds I listened to myself breathing in and out. It was like floating under water. When I was okay to sit up again, I noticed that Tim looked very, very pale. It could have been the moonlight, but I knew that it wasn't.

Quietly I asked him, "Are you okay, Tim?"

"No, no I'm not. That was really scary, Blythe. What just happened to you?"

"Oh that, I just fainted. It's okay, I'm fine, see?"

With that I stood up and tried to twirl around, but I began to wobble, so I had to sit back down.

"No, Blythe. I don't think you're fine, and you know you're not." Pride.

"Yes, Tim, I am fine. You said it yourself: you don't know me. I'll let you know when I need your help."

"I'm not saying that I'm the one to help you, but I do think you need to get some help."

"Guess what, Timmy boy: I've already had help. This *is* me with help. So just back off. Now go!"

"I'm not leaving you here in the middle of nowhere sitting in the dark."

"Oh yes you are. I told you I'm fine and now I want you to leave. If you want my notes, I think I left them in the cafeteria."

"Blythe, I'm not here to get your notes. Let me just walk you back to the dorm."

"No! I said leave me alone! If you don't I'll scream and there's bound to be some noble farmer out here somewhere with his trusty shotgun."

"Fine, be stubborn about it, but if you're not back at the dorm in an hour, I'm sending out the entire campus security squad to *drag* you back."

Now I had managed to get Tim all riled up, and it takes a lot to get his temper going. He stomped off, and I sat there for a minute very pleased with myself. Finally I stood up and began to brush the hair out of my eyes. That's when I realized I had lost my headband. In a fury I decided I was not going back to the dorm until I found it. I think I covered every square inch of that cornfield, but a black headband is not the easiest object to spot at night. When I finally got back to the dorm, Tim was sitting on the brick wall with a smirk on his face.

"Well look what the cat dragged in," he said.

"That's something my Grandma would say."

"Your Grandma must be a very wise woman."

"Shut up."

I gave him the best glare I could manage while picking grass out of my hair. If he wants to worry about me, I'll just have to give him something to worry about. I'm running twice as much tomorrow.

4.13.98

Weight: 100

I can't believe I haven't lost any weight in three days! I'm leaving on Sunday, and I've been running twice as much as usual and eating twice as little. God is against me again. What did I ever do to Him? I made the mistake of reading my Bible today:

> Now listen, you who say, "Today or tomorrow we will go to this or that city, spend a year there, carry on business and make money." Why, you do not even know what will happen tomorrow. What is your life? You are a mist that appears for a little while and then vanishes. Instead, you ought to say, 'If it is the Lord's will, we will live and do this or that.' As it is, you boast and brag. All such boasting is evil. Anyone, then, who knows the good he ought to do and doesn't do it, sins.
>
> JAMES 4:13-17

Can you believe that?! He just threw that in my face. It's not like I don't know He doesn't want me to do what I'm doing, but does He have to say that my life is worth nothing? I know He's mad at me because I'm fighting Him, but isn't that what we all do while we're on this planet "for a little while and then vanish"? We spend the entire time fighting the One who made us. It's in my nature, so just leave me alone. Wasn't it Camus who said,

> I do not want to believe that death is the gateway to another life. For me, it is a closed door. I do not say it is a step we all must take, but that it is a horrible and dirty adventure.

Even *he* realized that life is about living for oneself. Sure, I could wake up every day saying, "I will get up and brush my teeth now, if God wills it," but I don't wish to live a simpering life, never taking a solid step, always trembling.

And I don't think God wants me to live that way either. I choose to live my life to the fullest and make it my own. I have set goals for myself which I intend to fulfill, and if God doesn't like that, then He can stop me, but I'm not simply going to give in because He says so.

4.14.98

Weight: 100 (Still! Argh!)

The Heat

It's cold here.
The people are cold.
I'm warm,
I'm hot,
Nobody here cares.
Unthawable, unthinkable,
I'm hot.
Hospital corners,
A sterile bed.
I'm too hot.
They stare and point
With perfect hands
At my heat
That destroys their . . .
Hospital corners.
They whisper,
Icy breaths make puffy clouds,
A sinister chill.
They hate the heat.
They hate me.
I'm too hot.
The sweat,
It's dirty . . .
To them,
To the blue ones,
The numb.
It's too much.

I'm too much.
But I can't turn it down.
The heat keeps coming.
I'm burning a hole,
A hole through myself.

That's how I feel about this place. They all stare now. I feel them looking at me and talking behind my back. Tim has said something; I know it. He is a traitor. I thought I loved him, but all he has done is cause me grief. I haven't talked to him since that night. He has tried, but my pride won't let me respond. He needs to know that he can't fix me, that I'm not broken.

I'm tired, and I'm ready to go home. Not for my parents' sake, but for mine. This place is too rough on me. I have bruises from the brick walk and the edges of the sharp plastic chairs. The bed is too hard, and my hip bones won't let me lay out anymore because it hurts to lay on my stomach. The world I came from was soft. This world is too sharp, and I'm ready to leave. I've just got to hang on until tomorrow. I've made a list of all the foods that I'm going to eat when I get home:

- cinnamon rolls the size of my hand from the bakery down the street, no icing, I hate icing
- barbeque chips with the hottest salsa I can find
- Mom's egg salad on wheat bread
- the mini-chocolate-chip cookies with pecans that Mom buys from the store
- a blueberry bagel with cream cheese and strawberry jam
- an ice cream cake with mint chocolate chip ice cream on top of chocolate cake

- *trail mix from the store where you can mix a ton of kinds together*
- *a Snickers ice cream bar*
- *cranberry-orange bread, the yeast kind, not the cake kind*

I'm not sure I'm going to be able to eat all this in twenty-four hours, but I'm sure going to do my best. I'm going to start with Mom's egg salad, because it will make her happy if I let her fix something for me and she can see me eat it. When I've eaten a decent meal in front of the parents, I think I'll sneak a few of these items to my room so I can watch television, which I haven't done in a month, and eat, which I also haven't really done in a month.

I can eat more if I have the television on. I don't know why. This was how I ate when I was supposed to gain weight and everyone thought I was fine. It's a method that's been tested and perfected, and it's known to be foolproof.

Writing all this stuff down makes my stomach hurt. It's easier if I lie down. I can handle the dizziness better lying down. And the diet drinks aren't really working as much as they used to—the bubbles sting rather than fulfill. None of my clothes really fit me anymore, so I've had to shrink a lot of my stuff. It's hard work, keeping everyone else from worrying.

The good news is that everything is working in my favor for the return home. I've talked Mom into picking me up alone, so Dad doesn't have a chance to plan a hiking adventure. I don't think I could make it without stumbling or falling, and I can't wear shorts right now because of the bruises. Everything will be better when I get home.

Oliver said he's throwing me a welcome home party, and Diane is doing the decorations. I'm *so* ready to see them both.

Oliver said he has lots to tell me, but I have to wait until it's just the two of us. He's so crazy. He likes to make a production out of things just as much as I do.

Well, Tim is making his way over here, and if I don't get up now I'm in danger of actually having a conversation with him. This would all be easier if he weren't so cute and charming.

4.16.98

I am too weak! I decide I am not going to have anything to do with a guy, and then all he has to do is smile and I'm back to slush.

It happened after classes today, and I was sitting on the grass behind the dorm. It was nice outside and I was lying on my back looking up at the sky thinking about home when a shadow fell across my face. I shut my eyes to it, hoping it would go away, but it only intensified as Tim leaned over me.

"Are you okay, Blythe?"

"Yes, I'm okay. You know I can lie on the ground without having first fainted to get there."

"Okay, sorry. I was just coming to talk to you."

An exasperated sigh escaped me.

"Haven't we had enough serious conversations to last a lifetime?"

"It's nothing serious, I promise."

I propped up on my elbows and looked at him. He was pulling at blades of grass and not looking at me. He looked sweet, almost embarrassed.

"Okay, what then?"

"Well, you know there's a dance tomorrow night."

"Yeah I know."

"I guess I was wondering if you would want to meet up with me at 7:30 so we could go in together."

"Why, so you can keep an eye on me?"

"No . . . yes . . . well, sort of . . . but not in that way."

He looked up at me then down again, embarrassed. I kept a straight face, though I wanted to smile back.

"We'll see. I'll come if I can."

He was about to say something, but I stood up, brushed the grass from my jeans and walked inside without looking back. I was not going to go through another Owen incident. I had to keep this one on his toes.

4.18.98

You won't believe what happened at the dance last night! I had decided to wear this khaki skirt that hit at midshin with a split up the front and a yellow blouse. I clipped my hair back, put a little mascara on, and I was ready to roll. (No matter that the outfit I had picked out four weeks ago was a little too loose and the skirt kept sliding down.) Also, if I was an average B cup before I got to Nerd Academy USA, I had definitely been downsized to a pitiful A. I couldn't believe it! I had been wearing sports bras for so long I didn't notice that my normal ones were a little loose. Oh well, I thought, maybe Tim likes that kind of girl.

Boy was I wrong.

I arrived at the dance fashionably late. My stomach was in knots; this was the first thing Tim and I had done on anything but a professional level. And I was taking a chance on him, hoping he wouldn't turn out like Owen. I was to meet him outside the gym at half-past seven.

I came at a quarter till eight, but he was nowhere in sight. After about five minutes I began to worry about him. *What if he had fallen in the shower at the dorm and there was no one to help?* Or worse, *what if he had been kidnapped?* I know he's sixteen and not a kid, but it's been known to happen.

I was prepared to run to the dorms to see if he was okay when I heard his laughter spilling out the gym doors and into the muggy night. Slowly, I turned and walked as calmly as I could toward the building that leaked neon lights and manufactured fog. I saw his silhouette, black against the brightness of artificial light. I was no longer fearful for his safety. Now I was angry. He was dancing with some girl whom I refused to look at. My business was with him, not the one he chose over me.

Cool and collected, I walked up and tapped him on the shoulder. This is what came of it:

MORGAN MENZIE

"Hey, Blythe! What's up?"

Calmly, "We were supposed to meet."

"What? I can't hear you over all this music."

That's when I grabbed him and pulled him outside.

"Maybe you can hear me a little better now. I thought you were going to meet me, and we were going to the dance together."

"Yeah, I know and I was here, but you were late and it was never definite, and Lacy asked me to dance so I . . ."

"Why didn't you wait for me?"

"You're the one who has made it very clear that you want nothing to do with me. Every time I try to talk to you, you get mad and walk away."

"Well, I . . . I just wasn't sure how to handle you."

He softened a bit and I could tell he had forgotten about Lacy. He put his hand on my shoulder.

"If you're worried about me telling anyone what happened the other night, I won't. I promise, I won't tell anyone you're sick."

"I am *not* sick!" I jerked away from him. "And where do you get off thinking you're so superior? You think you were doing me a favor tonight, going to the dance with me? Well you're wrong. I was doing *you* the favor. I mean, you seem so inept at social gatherings."

"Come on, Blythe; I hate to see you mad. I didn't mean anything by it. I just want you to know that you can trust me. What's a little spat between friends? Let's forget about this whole thing, and I'll sweep you off your feet."

"I don't think so, Tim. I don't need your *sympathy* dance."

"Blythe, it's not a sympathy anything. When will you get it that I just like you? I like you, not because I feel sorry for you or to patronize you, but just because I like you."

"That's not true."

"What do you mean?"

"If you really knew me you wouldn't like me. If you knew the real me, you wouldn't like me at all."

"How do you know if you won't let me try?"

"It's just safer this way. It's easier for both of us this way."

"Easier for you, you mean."

"I'm tired. I think I'll be going back to the dorm now."

"Don't walk away, Blythe."

I didn't have enough breath to say more. I couldn't fake another smile. It took all my strength to hold in the tears until I got out of earshot. I ran back to the room, trying not to go back over everything he had said, trying not to let it sink in.

And this was how I left it. I never gave him my address, and I hope I never see him again. Boys like him and Owen are a waste of my time. At least Owen never dared challenge me.

All of a sudden I desperately missed Oliver. I wanted to tell him what happened, and I wanted him to tell me that everything was okay. But when I got back to the dorm, he didn't answer his phone so I went to bed early, pretending I couldn't hear the music pouring out of those doors. Since sleep was out of the question, I sat up the rest of the night, pretending the growling in my stomach was aimed at Tim and conjuring up all sorts of wicked names for him.

The next morning during the assembly I noticed Lacy, the girl Tim had taken up with. She wasn't beautiful by any means. She looked a bit overweight to me. Of course, she was curvy in a way I'd never be. Oh sure, Tim never judged a girl by her looks. Yeah, right.

So that was my send-off from the Academy, which I choose never to think about again. I told Erin that I would write, but I doubt I will unless home proves as dissatisfying as this month.

5.2.98

Weight: 100 (even after pigging out!)

Hooray! Hooray! I'm home! I'm home! I never really understood Dorothy's sentiment until now; there really is no place like home. Besides, for me this world is more black and white than any I've ever imagined.

Dad did end up coming. Mom said he wanted to be at the ceremony. We have this dumb presentation thing at the end, where we get medals for graduating. I like to think of them as achievement medals for the pounds I have shed. It actually wasn't that bad having him come. On the car ride back I ate the candy I was given in front of them, so as to ease two minds at once.

There was just one snag. He decided to stop for a bite to eat. This of course was not in my plans. I had already called Mom two days in advance to make sure she had made the egg salad, which was to be the *first* course in my new food voyage. How could he do this to me when I had almost made it?

I pretended to be asleep when we stopped in hopes of being left in the car to rest. Unfortunately, they decided I was too young to be left alone in the car, no matter how many times I sarcastically pointed out that I wasn't too young to be left alone with a bunch of crazy strangers for a month.

I was so angry by the time we went into whatever old-people cafeteria Dad had chosen that I sat on the edge of my chair the entire time, refusing to look at either Mom or Dad or to order anything but water. At least they thought that I didn't order anything because I was mad. How would I ever have explained my celebration day of food to them? They weren't even understanding enough to leave me in the car to fake sleep!

5.3.98

It's good to be home. It seems full of the atmosphere I had so desperately missed. Mom and I immediately went to Grandma and Pa's, and I hugged them both so long I thought we were permanently glued together. It wasn't until then that I noticed how uncomfortable it was to be hugged. I had gone a month without them, and now they felt awkward and Grandma seemed to engulf me. I felt my hips digging into her grandmotherly stomach while she patted my back, right on my shoulder blades where I tried to flattened them out as much as I could.

She clucked her tongue audibly and looked at Mom. I pulled away as fast as I could. Pa was a little easier; he was about as bony as I was. We fit together like building blocks. He laughed in my ear and whispered, "Don't worry about your Grandma, she just wants what's best for you. I know you're fit as a fiddle." With that he let me go, and I felt the first pang of guilt since I started my self-improvement.

It was the first time I felt like I was doing something wrong.

Note to self: Figure out what's wrong with me and decide if my eating patterns prove ill.

MORGAN MENZIE

5.10.98

In light of Tim's incorrigible behavior, I have been compelled to write another letter to my future husband. This letter highlights the fact that I have not found Mr. Wonderful yet:

My Love,

I've tried calling you on the phone, just to see, but it's never you who picks up. I've tapped you on the shoulder in the bookstore to see what you like to read, but it's never your face that looks up. I've stared at you in class, waiting for you to speak, but your voice comes out all wrong.

I won't give up, my love. I can't, for I feel you rushing past me like a whisper in the wind, and I feel you watching me as I try to sleep at night.

You're out there somewhere . . . somewhere far away from me, and God is calling us. He's holding my hand and yours until one day He can place them together palm to palm. He'll kiss our foreheads and bless our souls as we catch a glimpse of heaven in each other's eyes.

Love,
Me

That's all I've got so far, just two letters and a whole lot of dreams. I think I'm okay about Tim now. He's not always on my mind anymore. I think God has taken him out of my thoughts so I can have some peace. I must not be doing anything wrong after all.

5.20.98

Weight: 95

I finally got around to unpacking. It's been almost a month since I've been home, and I've been living out of my suitcase. Even though I'd been at a regular college campus, all my clothes smelled like camp—you know, like mildewed toothpaste.

You're not going to believe what I found in one of the pockets of my suitcase: a letter from Tim. Here's what it said:

Dear Blythe,

I know I need to apologize for last night. I'm sorry I hurt your feelings. I'm sorry I was just being stupid, and I'm sorry I couldn't see what you needed. I really hate to hurt people's feelings, especially yours.

I guess some of the reason I didn't want to give up on finding out what was upsetting you was because you seem like a cool girl, and I just wanted to interact and get to know you. I just wanted to be in your life very badly. Sorry if that seemed too forward. I know we haven't known each other long, but I can't help caring about you.

I felt so stupid after I saw how upset I had made you when you showed up and I wasn't there waiting for you at the dance. And then I tried to fix it by turning on you when I should have just left you alone. You have your reasons for what you do, and it is none of my business. I felt very ashamed, and I should've been. I left the dance right away and wrote this note.

Please try to forgive me and try to realize that I didn't mean to hurt you.

Tim

On the back was his address. You can imagine how taken aback I was. I mean, I had labeled and stamped *insensitive* on Tim's forehead, and now he goes and does something like this. In the story in my head, I'm a career girl who has too much in my life to worry about romance. I have a career to balance (school), and I have a whole mess of personal issues that keeps me from opening up, and now, he comes along and shatters all my practicalities with one note! No! Absolutely not!

I am not going to give up my plan and my dreams just so some guy can be a jerk to me whenever he feels like it! And then apologize only to hurt me again later. I am *not,* and I repeat *not* going to write him. He can wither up in his own pool of tears for all I care. No one is allowed to hurt me again, no matter how good his apology is.

I think I'll go call Oliver now.

6.5.98

Weight: 92 (feelin' sexy)

Oliver and I went to dinner tonight. It was so fun. I hadn't realized how much I'd missed him. He can always make me laugh, yet he has a way about him that lets you know when he's sincere. He's not one who can fake emotions. He's been known to try, but I can always call him on it.

We decided to get dressed up and go somewhere nice. I wore a light blue v-neck shirt and a linen skirt with embroidery along the bottom in rich maroon and blue flowers. He said I looked great. Although I didn't tell him, because for some reason I got shy, he looked good, too. He was wearing khakis and a pale blue oxford shirt that matched his eyes, and he had the sleeves rolled up just enough to where I could tell he'd been out working at his parents' farm; he was barely golden. Oliver's tan was always more gold than bronze. That's what he gets for having blond hair and blue eyes.

But I like it. It was familiar and sweet.

We went downtown for dinner and ate out on a screened-in deck. The music was playing, and the breeze was warm but not oppressive. It was lovely. I gave him his birthday present; I had been away when he turned sixteen. We shared a dessert and then went for a drive, now that he had his license. We rode all around the old, rich neighborhoods that made up the outskirts of town before you get to the country, where we live. Me, in my predictable suburban colonial home and him in his southern-boy farmhouse. We talked about old times with the windows down, and I laughed at his choice of music. That's how we are. We tease each other with affection. Later we went for a walk in the woods near my house.

It was a wonderful night.

MORGAN MENZIE

He took me back to my house to drop me off, and I waved to him until he rounded the bend like I was never going to see him again. I went to bed very happy tonight—happier than I've been in a long time. It is good to have a friend like Oliver.

1:00 A.M. I heard a tapping on my window. Convinced that I was hallucinating from my insomnia, I shut my eyes and tried to ignore it. After all, I live on the second story; who or what would possibly be tapping on my window? When it refused to stop, and I had checked my vitals to make sure that everything was in working order, I carefully walked to the window. Opening the shutters very carefully, I peeked outside.

There was Oliver, waving like a madman for me to come down. Quickly I pulled my blue terry cloth robe over my white cotton nightgown. I was down in a flash. I couldn't imagine what was so urgent that he had to talk to me now. I was afraid he had woken my parents.

We sat on the front steps for what seemed like forever in silence while I nervously kept tucking my robe around my waist and under my legs. I felt like a whale in it, and like I was too exposed. Oliver just sat there like a stunned rabbit, neither moving nor breathing for all I could tell. Finally, I broke the silence and asked him what I could do for him:

"What's going on, Oliver? Are you okay?"

"Yeah, yeah I'm fine. I guess I just wanted to talk to you."

"We just saw each other a few hours ago. Couldn't we talk in the morning?"

"What I have to say I sorta gotta say now."

"What's the matter? You sound so serious."

"Okay, here it goes. I've been thinking about us a lot lately, and I missed you more than I thought when you were gone."

"Me too."

"Good, because I think I like you. I mean, I think I like you more than a friend. I have more fun with you than I do with anybody else, and I was wondering if you want to go out. You know, if we could give it a try."

"I—"

"But I don't want to do it if it is going to ruin our friendship. I just think that it could be something more. We just, you know, go together."

With that, all thoughts of Tim went out the window.

"Oh Oliver, this is—"

"Now you don't have to say anything right now; you can just think about it for a while. But it was me who sent you the kisses, not Owen, and I've liked you for awhile and I had to tell you tonight when I got up the nerve."

"Well I think—"

"This doesn't mean the end of anything. It just means the beginning of something else, you know, something that could be good for both of us. And it drove me crazy to see you go after a guy like Owen when you're too good for him. I know neither of us has dated anyone, but who better to start with than each other? I know you wanted me to go out with Diane, but we just don't match. And you know that you and I go great together and . . ."

Laughing, "If you would just let me answer you! I think we should give it a try. We make such perfect friends; we're bound to make a perfect couple, right?"

"That's exactly what I was thinking. Whew, I'm so glad you agree. I was so nervous. By the way, did you know that you have absolutely no rocks in your yard. I searched for about fifteen minutes in the dark and couldn't find a single one."

"Then what did you throw at my window?"

This is when he got really embarrassed. "I sorta threw quarters. They were all I had."

"You threw money at my window? That's great! I don't know if I can date someone who tried to buy me!"

"Ha ha! . . . (serious face) You're kidding, right?"

"Of course I'm kidding!"

And that was how Oliver and I started dating. I was in a daze when I got back from going out. Then I went straight to bed and lay there until the ceiling started to swirl like it always does when my body decides that I should be sleeping.

But now I'm wide awake and it's going on 3:00 A.M. I wonder what it's going to be like when school starts? Could Oliver be the love that I've been writing to in my letters? It's so perfect now that I think about it! The man I'm supposed to marry has been right under my nose all along; I just had to truly see him for the first time.

It's so romantic.

9.1.98

Weight: 92

First Day of Junior Year

This was supposed to be a great year and now it's ruined. I actually have a boyfriend, and Diane and I are in almost every class together, but it doesn't matter now.

Oliver and I were going to meet on the stairs outside of school before first period. I had gotten up at 5:00 A.M. and had gone to work out, and I was right on time to meet him at 6:30. I was looking over my class schedule and making notes to myself in my day planner. I was so engrossed in the task that Oliver completely took me by surprise when he tapped on my shoulder.

I jumped up and watched as the world around me darkened, and that all-too-familiar cold sweat broke out on my neck. I watched the ground rise up to meet me.

Apparently Oliver is not as quick as Tim, for I was lying there as blood slowly dripped from a long cut just above my right eye. As I stared at the dep crimson evidence of life on the tips of my fingers, I realized I had fallen smack onto the concrete steps. When the feeling came back into my arms and legs and I could sit up, I began to cry.

Poor Oliver didn't know what was going on. He just kept saying, "Oh, oh don't cry. You'll be okay. Let me go get you a paper towel." He didn't understand that I wasn't crying from the pain. I was crying from the fall that symbolized the pit of destruction I had dug for myself. I couldn't explain it to him, and I didn't really feel like trying. I just quietly asked him to drive me to the hospital.

Oliver could not stop talking in the car on the drive to the emergency room. I knew it was because he was nervous, and because I knew he really wasn't expecting a reply, I drifted into a melancholy daze. My head felt very light, like a balloon on a string. I was half leaning out the window in a feeble attempt to keep the blood from getting on his car.

I didn't notice the exact point at which I began to hum. It wasn't until we pulled up to the hospital entrance and Oliver helped me out of the car that I realized I had been humming "Jesus Loves Me." From the moment I could remember, I had always sung this song when I was afraid.

When I was little and I had to get allergy shots, I would sing this song in my head to keep from watching the needle. When I had to have my tonsils out, I sang this song as I drifted under the wave of anesthetic. And once again, on my sixteenth birthday, I was humming the same tune.

The stitches weren't that bad. Just five neat X's that traversed the right half of my right eyebrow. The exaggerated arch gave the impression of constant surprise or slyness. I prefer slyness.

When Mom pulled up I was gingerly fingering the puffy cut. She looked like she'd been crying. She ran up and hugged me without saying a word. I could feel her grating my shoulder blades together, but at that moment it was a welcomed pain. I pushed her away from me and began the story I had rehearsed from the moment my head hit the pavement:

"Mom, I need to tell you something, and please don't interrupt me until I'm through because I have a lot to say.

"I am not well. In fact I don't think I was ever well. When you thought I was better, I simply weighed more. I was still as unhappy as ever. I just wanted you and Dad not to worry, so I ate and ate to get myself up to normal weight. But I lied on my food logs and didn't gain the weight the right way, and it only made things worse.

"When I went to Collins-Weatherby, I knew I was going to lose weight, but I didn't know it would get this out of hand. I hardly ate anything while I was there, and I weighed myself every day."

She was quiet. "I knew there was something wrong when I pulled that scale out of your bag. My stomach just turned."

"Mom, please let me finish. This isn't the first time I've fainted. It's been happening a lot, but I thought I could control it or at least it wouldn't affect anyone else. I'm just so miserable in my life and everything seems out of control. Most days I just want to curl back up in bed and ignore the world outside.

"Mom, I need help. And I hate feeling this way, and I cry all the time. Laurie, the girl that used to go to school with me who played soccer, gave me the number of this doctor downtown. I don't know why I kept it, but I did and I think I want to call him. Please don't be mad at me."

"Oh, Blythe, I'm not mad at you. I'm so glad you're getting help. I'm mad at myself for not recognizing the signs sooner. Your daddy has been bugging me since you got back this summer to get you some help again, but I just ignored him. I thought he was overreacting."

At this point she began to cry and could not utter another word, so we went home.

I wanted to go to school, but Dad thought we should all meet at home and talk about all this, and I didn't have the strength to fight him on it.

You don't need to hear exactly what was said. I can give you the gist in a few phrases: lots of crying, lots of hugging, and a little bit of yelling. Dad and I did most of the yelling. That fact that he knew what was going on the whole time made me furious, and I'm not sure why. I guess it's because I thought I was fooling everyone. I certainly fooled Mom, for all she did was cry and say how this was all her fault and how she should have gotten me help sooner.

I am going to see Dr. Bernhardt, the one Laurie recommended, next week. That's the soonest he could get me in, and I don't know if I can make it that long. It's like, now that I'm actually getting help for real, I want to get it *now*. You couldn't imagine how infuriated I was when Laurie slipped me the note with his name. I thought I was over letting her get to me, but instead of saying anything, I just slipped the paper in my gym bag. It was the end of our freshman year, and she was transferring to a different school, so I figured I'd just let it slide.

I wonder how she's doing?

Probably better than me.

9.2.98

I found this verse today:

> When I kept silent, my bones wasted away through my groaning all day long. For day and night your hand was heavy upon me; my strength was sapped as in the heat of summer. Then I acknowledged my sin to you and did not cover up my iniquity. I said, "I will confess my transgressions to the LORD"—and you forgave the guilt of my sin.
>
> PSALM 32:3-5

I think God is trying to tell me something. I hope He is trying to tell me that I will get better now, but I'm afraid to make a wish that big when I've been running from Him and hating Him for three years now?

No, I am not ready to hope that big yet.

MORGAN MENZIE

9.3.98

I saw the doctor today. I couldn't wait until next week. After ten minutes on the phone arguing with his nurse/secretary, she deemed me worthy of a breakdown and maneuvered his schedule to fit me in immediately. The world just seemed to be getting darker and darker, and I knew that if I didn't see him today, I would lose all nerve and escape back into safe bad habits.

So I skipped school. I figured my intelligence, though detrimental in the past, will buy me a one-day pass from classes. My parents did not know how desperately I needed to see him, and I begged Oliver to take me. Diane came too for moral support.

Oliver and Diane weren't allowed to come into the inner waiting room, so I sat there by myself waiting to be judged. Before I knew it I was in the throes of a panic attack. The room closed in on me and threatened to swallow me up. The nurses kept staring at me. I was so nervous that I couldn't stop crying, and I was breathing so fast that I couldn't control it. My brain just stopped working—fear radiated through my body like a chilled heat wave. I couldn't see very well through the haze of tears.

One of the nurses tried to hand me a tissue, but I shied away from her blurred image. When the time came to see the doctor, I had calmed down a bit and was concentrating on breathing as I climbed up on the industrial scale. They made me put on this huge hospital gown and stand on the scale backward, a sharp reminder of my visits with Becca. I felt the sterile cold air waft through the open slit in my gown and shivered.

A kind nurse then took my blood pressure, which she seemed worried about. She asked me when my last period was. A lie would have been the easy thing to do, but my brain had not thawed out from the panic attack so I just whispered, "three years ago."

I didn't look up. She patted my shoulder and left me alone.

Next came the doctor. Dr. Bernhardt.

"Blythe, I want to help you, but I can't do that unless I know that you really want to get better."

Scaldingly, "Of course I want to get better!"

"You say that, but right now your body and emotions are in crisis mode, and it is our natural instinct as humans to get ourselves as quickly as possible out of danger. What I need to know is if you are still going to fight this disease once you have passed the crisis point. Because, from what I can tell of your records, you're good at fooling those around you into thinking you are better."

Hurt, humbled, "But I thought I *was* better."

"Then you fool yourself, too, but you must be completely honest with me in order for me to help you. I suggest you see a psychologist and I am prescribing a low dosage of Zoloft, because I feel that in order for you to fight this, you must be able to see that it is not impossible. Right now you feel . . ."

He continued to talk, but I had ceased to listen at the word *Zoloft*. My defenses had instinctively drawn up, and I closed myself to the outside world. This didn't fit in to The Plan. People like me didn't need *medication*. For heaven's sake, I am not crazy or suicidal. I am just a reasonable person seeking a reasonable plan, and this sounded very unreasonable. As if the idea of some Freudian psychologist suggesting all my problems are rooted in sexual angst didn't upset me enough! He just needed to give me a little room and a little warmth to allow my brain to heat up and find a way out of this. His drugs will make me slow and steal all my emotions from me.

He is trying to take all that I am away from me! What will my family think? The academy is a regular rumor mill—there's nothing a good Christian school loves more than a bit of juicy gossip. I never cared what they thought before, because I was always superior, but this medication will lower me to their level, or perhaps even lower! Why did I think he could help me?

When I was finally dismissed, I ran to Diane and cried until there were no more tears left. I was exhausted, and now I had to go tell Mom and Dad what the doctor said. Of course he was probably talking to them right this minute, luring them into his net of deception, making them think I needed his healing powers, telling Mom this medicine would make me less dramatic and be able to enjoy life more.

Yeah well, I don't want my dramatics taken away from me, and I don't want more joy. I just want to be left alone!

Oliver took me back to my house. We drove in silence. At home I told Mom that I had been to see the doctor today, and that he wanted to meet with her and Dad. She seemed so startled about my skipping school that I believe Dr. Bernhardt kept his word and allowed me to tell her myself.

Maybe he's not as bad as I thought.

I couldn't go to sleep that night. The doctor's words kept running through my mind, and all the horrible scenes from the last three years flashed before my eyes as I fingered the cut above my eye. Finally, I got down on my knees beside my bed like I used to when I was little.

I didn't say anything for a long time. I just sat there, not thinking, but letting my mind absorb what the doctor had said. The silence wrapped around me like a warm cloak and stopped my shaking.

I began to cry. The tears were for all the years I had lost and the future I could not see ahead. They were for the hurt I had caused my parents and friends. They were for the denial I had built up like a fortress around me. And they were for the doctor, who in his infinite kindness had shaken me out of my apathy.

As the pain and bitterness flowed from me, I sank to the

ground, rocking slightly back and forth to feel the warm air brush past my face. Still, I did not say anything. I just let His hand rest on me. Much later I whispered "thank you" and fell asleep on the floor.

9.30.98

It's been a month since my first visit to Dr. Bernhardt. My life has begun to change: Oliver and I broke up last week.

Actually he broke up with me, but I guess it was the right thing to do. It's strange. I'm not going to miss him. I mean, it hurt when he told me we ought to be friends. It hurt very badly, but it was more from the breaking of my pride than of attachment to him. We were dating out of comfort rather than desire. I know he is right, but I hate him for it. And I hate myself for hating him for it.

I told Katherine about him in my first visit; she's my therapist/psychologist. For the first time in my life I have someone to talk to who listens with her heart *and* mind. She is not my best friend or ex-boyfriend or parent, and I love that. I trust her. I trust her more than I trust myself. And I'm putting myself in her hands.

I've studied her just as she studies me. She doesn't look at all like what I had imagined. You could never forget Katherine. She's in her late thirties tops and has sleek, brown hair without a gray one in sight. She doesn't own old-lady clothes, and she curls up in her chair like I do. She's lanky like a cat with pronounced features that on anyone else would seem overstated, but on her look Grecian.

She is not a Freud-wielding fanatic as I thought. She is kind and speaks honestly and firmly. She speaks to me of a future I could not imagine on my own, and she has faith in me that I will be able to see it, too. Her candor surprises me and frustrates me and makes me believe her. She will never mislead me or belittle me. The deceptions that I use on myself and my world end the minute I step through her door. She has the power to look at me and glean the truth from the lies. All in all, she reminds me of the kind of person I want to be when I grow up.

I feel so blessed to have her in my life. God has placed her here to lead me to where He wants me to be. She understands me in a way no one ever has before, and she knows what I mean when I try to tell her things. She has a gift for understanding people, and God knew that I needed someone with a highly tuned sensitivity to understand how I work. She sees how I view the world and therefore can help me see it in a more healthy way.

We talked out my split from Oliver. She says it's perfectly normal to feel hurt even if I agreed with every word he said. She says that it doesn't matter if it was the right decision or not, it still hurts because in the end I did get dumped. (I wish I knew more doctors who are confident enough to use the word *dump* without losing their dignity.)

She says that the hurt I feel comes from my emotions that were wrapped up in my relationship with Oliver and that I should not try to reason them away. It's a good feeling to know that I don't have to be practical all the time. I can just be upset if I want to because that's what I feel. It just goes to show how far I was down the wrong road when any emotion at all feels foreign to me. I was so numbed with food, or absence thereof, that feelings were a luxury for which I did not have room.

What's surprised me the most about the last month in my life is the fear that has grown inside me. Living in my thoughts for the last few years has cultivated a fear of anything in the real world. I am afraid of meeting new people, of doing less than excellent in school, of having fun, of talking to my parents, of being in any kind of relationship, and of getting to know myself. I'm afraid of what I might find, but I've got to look or I'll never really live.

| 1999 |

12.20.99

Christmas Break

Well, it's Christmas, my favorite time of the year, and I am seventeen years old and in full recovery. I know I haven't written in over a year, but something made me pick this journal back up. Pa died a couple of weeks ago.

I haven't ever seen Grandma cry before, but that day I saw enough tears to last me a lifetime. I had hardly spent one full day with them since I got sick, because it was easier not to deal with them. And now Pa is gone and I can never get that time back. I can never dance with him across the living room floor, and he'll never get to see me well.

I asked God to tell Pa that I'm not going to let him down. I am not stopping in my recovery. It is always a push and pull situation with my eating disorder when something in my life goes bad, but I am not falling back. Pa would not have wanted it that way.

I'm trying to cheer Grandma up as much as I can. I give her lots of hugs and love on her as much as she'll let me. She tends to isolate herself when she gets sad. Looks like I take after her more than I thought. I've started going over to her house and letting her cook for me. She gets so excited, and I think it does us both good.

She told me the story of how she and Pa got married. (I've found that I am a better listener now that my own worries aren't constantly buzzing in my head.) She was only eighteen and he was in the Civilian Conservation Corps. Young men who belonged to the CCC weren't supposed to get married, but he had always been a rebel, so he married Grandma on the side of the road in Oklahoma before he left to work with the other men. They didn't see each other for three months. They loved each other with a devotion that only they could see.

It's snowing outside. Everything's turning white. Suburbia doesn't seem quite so bad with the sameness paved over in icy flakes. It's warm in the house. Dad has built a fire and his Christmas Billboard Hits CD is playing in the background. I'm warmer than I've felt in a long time—the warmth from a place that only healing can kindle.

$$\Big|\ 2000\ \Big|$$

1.1.00

I spent New Year's with my family. Mom and Dad and I played cards and drank hot cider and listened to music until around eleven. Then Dad got it in his head that he wanted to go for a walk. Mom refused to go, but I was up for it and wanted a chance to talk to Dad alone, so we headed out, bundled in scarves and mittens and ski jackets.

I could see my breath on the air and condensing on the top layer of my scarf as we set out. For once Dad didn't hurry, but walked slowly and looked up at the stars. It was so clear and beautiful. I felt my heart wanting to tell him something.

He looked at me a little embarrassed and then asked, "So how are you, Blythe?"

I was still looking at the sky, and I smiled at the nervousness in his voice. I said, "Oh, I'm better than I've been in a long time. I'm happy."

"That's great, honey. That's really great."

His voice was a little shaky, so I turned to look at him.

"How are you, Dad?"

He sniffed a little.

"I'm real good, honey. I'm just real happy for you—for all of us. We're a very blessed family."

"Yeah, we are."

I took his hand, and we began walking again. I wasn't cold. I was excited—my heart knew something good was about to happen.

We got to the end of our road and turned around to walk back. The moon shone full through the tress now, lighting our path. Dad began to speak again.

"I got your card, Blythe. You said a lot."

"Oh . . . I had a lot to tell you."

"I've never gotten anything like that before."

"Is that good or bad?"

His voice started to shake and he took his hand away to pull out a tissue and blow his nose.

"It was good. It was very, very good. I've never been able to talk to you that easily. I just never know what to say. I read your letter and felt like I saw you for the first time." He stopped for a minute. "I love you, Blythe. You will always be my special angel."

He didn't say anything else. He couldn't.

"I love you too, Dad."

He took my hand again and we hurried on as Mom yelled from the house that the ball was about to drop.

I didn't make a list this year. I'm content with what I have right now.

3.3.00

Well, it's almost spring break. Since we'll be at different colleges next year, Diane and I are spending it together. It's not just a little frightening to think of going off to school somewhere far away with people I don't know, especially when I'm still in recovery. I know that all I've talked about since seventh grade was going off to school somewhere away from all the people I know. But now that I am able to love them I don't want to leave them. I know I will go and it will be hard at first, just like everything that's new and scary, but I also know I'll get over it and it will be wonderful and fresh and new, yet I'm sad. I'm sad that I put my parents through all these hard years and that I will be leaving them soon to enjoy my happiness after inflicting so much pain. Katherine says there is no use in looking back and wishing, and I know this is true; but everyone has regrets and those wasted years are a few of mine.

But I'm done feeling sorry for the old Blythe. She was from the past, and she has gone to a better place. All the drama that I create around my life is full of joy and excitement now. I want to share it with those I love. I am working on adding wisdom to my intellect and I thank my God every day for blessing me with insight and depth. Yet no matter how deep, the new Blythe will always have her superfluous laugh that is infectious in its tone and volume, because Kesey was right in *One Flew Over the Cuckoo's Nest* when he wrote that "you can't really be strong until you see a funny side to things."

The new Blythe loves to paint and wants to play the cello. She is stronger than she ever thought she could be. And she will always love God, because even as she slapped Him in the face, He put His hand on her and loved her through the worst of her life.

2.21.06

Dear Little One,

I found this journal last week as I was searching for my old toy chest to furnish your room. It has been ages since I've seen it. You kicked when I spotted it, so I know it was meant for you. Your great grand-father William made the cover with his own hands. You never got to meet him, but he was a wonderful man who knew how to enjoy life.

This journal describes the years of my life that made me the person I am. My faith exists because of this journey, and you exist as a testimony that miracles are possible and life is as wonderful and rich as you believe it can be.

Looking back, I suppose Collis-Weatherby wasn't all bad. After all, I did meet your father there. Of course we didn't reunite until college. When you're sick, it's hard to give enough of yourself to be in a relation-ship, but that is a whole other story. Someday I hope to gain the courage to tell it to you.

I will love you forever.

Your mother,
Blythe

Appendices

Approaching Someone You Suspect Has an Eating Disorder

Before you approach someone you suspect has an eating disorder, I would highly recommend that you educate yourself. Too many people believe that eating disorders are only about food and weight issues, when in reality, those are just the symptoms of underlying problems. Below is a list of some things to keep in mind when approaching someone.

- Avoid talking about food and weight; those are not the real issues.
- Assure them that they are not alone and that you love them and want to help in any way you can.
- Encourage them to seek help.
- Never try to force them to eat.
- Do not comment on their weight or appearance.
- Do not blame the individual and do not get angry with them.
- Be patient; recovery takes time.
- Do not make mealtimes a battleground.
- Listen to them; do not be quick to give opinions and advice.
- Do not take on the role of a therapist.

It is important to remember that when you first approach the person you suspect has an eating disorder, they may react with anger or they may deny that anything is wrong. Do not push the issue, just let them know that you will always be there for them if they need to talk. In cases where the person is extremely underweight or is bingeing/purging several times a day, you may need to step in and take control. I would only recommend doing that if the individual's health is in extreme danger. If that is the case, you may need to speak to a doctor about a forced hospitalization.

Watching people you love slowly kill themselves can be frightening. You will probably experience feelings of distress, anger, guilt, and confusion. No matter how much you want to help them, you must remember that only they can make the decision to get help. You cannot force them to do this.

Nutritional Information

A healthy teenage girl should be consuming at least 2,200 calories and 66 fat grams per day. While it is important to exercise, you should do no more than one hour of noncontinuous exercise per day. Do not exercise if you aren't getting your recommended calories and fat intake.

If you are struggling with an eating disorder, please contact the National Association of Anorexia Nervosa and Associated Disorders at 1-847-831-3438 to talk with a counselor. Their business hours are 9:00 A.M. to 5:00 P.M. (CST).

Contact Morgan Menzie

If you would like to contact Morgan Menzie, e-mail her at *diaryofananorexicgirl@hotmail.com*.

To chat with others about this book, please visit www.transit books.com and log on to the Diary of an Anorexic Girl chat board.

Revolve

$14.99
Available Summer '03

Part Bible. Part teen culture 'zine. The New Testament gets a totally cool makeover. God's words take on a whole new meaning for teen girls—addressing everything from beauty secrets to personal problems to fun quizzes that build your faith.

Check out these books from Transit!

The Rules

How the 10 Commandments are relevant for your life

$10.99 US
Available July '03

Witnessing 101

How to share your faith without freaking out

$10.99 US
Available May '03

Mission: Africa

Take a vacation from everything you take for granted

$11.99 US
Available July '03

Support the DATA Agenda!

We at Transit support the work of the DATA (Debt, AIDS, Trade, Africa) organization in Africa. Every day more than 5,500 people die from the AIDS virus. And every day more than 1,700 children are infected with HIV. Six times more girls than boys are infected. We cannot stand by while this holocaust happens before our eyes without doing anything to help. This is the moment in history where we will face our humanity, our faith, and our commitment to God. We are commanded to love our neighbor. Africa is our neighbor. Will you help?

Log on to www.datadata.org to write a letter to the president, your senators, and your congressmen today! You could change the world.

LaVergne, TN USA
23 February 2011
217649LV00001B/3/P